WORKERS AGAINST RACISM

THE ROOTS OF RACISM

junius

Workers Against Racism
The roots of racism
1. Politics
1. Title
ISBN 0-950 8404-8-3

First published January 1985

Typeset by Junius Publications Ltd (TU)
Printed by Morning Litho Printers Ltd (TU)

BCM JPLTD
London WC1N 3XX

Contents

Introduction 5

1. What is racism? 10

2. Beneath the surface 18

3. Going public 26

4. As British as the Union Jack 37

5. Riding the storm 48

6. Divide and rule 58

7. The great evasion 71

8. The way ahead 80

Introduction

Racism is rampant throughout the Western world. Nowhere is this more apparent than in Britain. The institutions of British society are imbued with racism from top to bottom. Racism exerts an overwhelming influence over every aspect of the lives of black people.

Take an everyday example of British racism. In March 1984 Mrs Carole May, headmistress of St Paul's and All Hallows Church of England infants' school in Tottenham, North London, called in the police to question four black children between the ages of four and six. Mrs May was acting on her suspicions 'that they had money on them which they should not have' *(Caribbean Times,* 9 November 1984). Despite outraged protests from black parents, Mrs May's action was fully endorsed by the school's board of governors, by the Haringey Education Authority, the Church of England and the Department of Education and Science. The Department conceded that the headmistress's action was racist, but considered that under the circumstances it was a legitimate response. Parents who wanted to pursue the matter further were advised to seek redress under the Race Relations Act.

The principle that if you are black you are automatically a criminal suspect guides the conduct of all British state institutions from infants' schools to old people's homes, from playgrounds to prisons. Racism is not merely legitimate but an established norm. Mrs May is not working on her own. Over the past decade state agencies have set up a special network for the surveillance of black and immigrant workers.

The Home Office has established close relations with the police and the Department of Health and Social Security. The surveillance network includes organisations concerned with the provision of services such as education, housing, health and the registration of births and marriages.

The health service has become increasingly colour conscious. In many parts of the country black people are required to produce a passport before they can register with a doctor or be admitted for hospital treatment. Discrimination is also rife in the dole offices. A recent report produced by the Child Poverty Action Group showed that black claimants face harassment and intimidation. Many black claimants are denied payment for months while the Home Office looks into their immigration status (CPAG, *Double discrimination: a report on racism in social security,* June 1984).

Many local councils promote the image of a harmonious multi-racial community. Yet local councils — including left-wing Labour councils — are some of the worst offenders against the rights of black people. Black people have been asked to produce their passports in Southwark and Hackney before they can get on to the housing list or get the services of a social worker. In Camden in 1983 the registrar of marriages demanded that black couples produce their passports at their wedding ceremonies.

The British obsession with race has led to the authorities putting a virtual stop to the entry of black people into the country over the past decade. It has also led to the proliferation of restrictions and regulations governing the lives of black people in Britain. The authorities have created the spectre of 'the illegal immigrant' to justify the extension of a network of internal controls. The police organise periodic 'fishing' expeditions in which they round up black residents in a hostel or black workers in a sweatshop and check their credentials. In early 1984 police in Hackney picked up more than 100 Turkish workers in a mass raid. Almost half were subsequently deported.

Changes in the immigration rules have given the police extensive powers. The guidelines on their conduct are not a matter for public debate — they are left to the discretion of the Home Office. The police have powers to detain and question black suspects and to raid and search their homes or workplaces. The police are authorised to probe into the most intimate details of people's lives to ascertain whether a marriage is 'genuine'.

The state has an unquenchable thirst for information on immigrants and black people. The Data Protection Bill which is widely supported by defenders of traditional British liberties specifically excludes from its provisions information required for the purposes of immigration control. The Home Office can obtain information held on computer about any person whom the authorities suspect, rightfully or wrongfully, to come under the jurisdiction of immigration controls. This includes access to health and social security records, credit listings and bank accounts.

Legal and institutional racism has endowed everyday racism with respectability. Racist violence, once a taboo subject, is now widely discussed in the media. Despite the obligatory expressions of sympathy and concern, police toleration of racist violence means that in an area like East London racists can publicly organise their campaign of terror. They have nothing to fear from the forces of law and order — they can rely on the police to turn a blind eye. A recent Policy Studies Institute report on the Metropolitan Police showed that racist views are the norm inside the force.

Discrimination

Racial oppression denies black people their basic democratic rights. It also forces black people into the worst schools, housing and jobs. A recent Department of Employment study shows that black unemployment is double that among whites. Unemployment rates among men of West Indian origin are running at more than 20 per cent *(Employment Gazette,* June 1984). The trend towards the intensification of discrimination in the labour market is confirmed by a number of recently published reports.

The state-sponsored Policy Studies Institute recently published its third survey of race relations in Britain. It contrasted its findings in the eighties with its earlier studies in the seventies and found that there had been no improvement in the position of black people in education, housing, employment and the allocation of services. In fact, in many areas things had got worse. The survey provided evidence of widespread discrimination. For example, in housing the survey confirmed the tendency towards the concentration of black people in run down inner-city areas. Whereas 59 per cent of black people live in Greater London and the West Midlands, only 21 per cent of white people live in these areas. The survey summed up the inferior housing standards endured by black people:

> **'The properties occupied by black people are, overall, markedly inferior to those occupied by white people: they are smaller, and certainly more crowded; they are more often flats, and those flats allocated tend to be on higher floors; they rarely have access to a garden.' (Policy Studies Institute, *Black and white Britain*, 1984)**

In employment the Policy Studies Institute found that there had been no appreciable change in the position of black people since the fifties and sixties. Workers of Asian and West Indian origin are still segregated in the lowest paid sectors and work under the worst conditions. For example, just less than a third of all black men work shifts regularly, compared with a fifth of white men. The survey found that on average white men earn £20 a week more than West Indians and £18 a week more than Asians. The only significant change noted over the past 10 years was that unemployment had grown more rapidly among blacks:

'On balance we conclude from our comparison of the 1974 and 1982 surveys and our analysis of individual jobs and job movements that the British job market has changed little in its hostility to black workers, except that now it excludes more of them from work altogether.'

A recent study of the involvement of black youth in the government's Youth Training Scheme confirms the Policy Studies Institute's conclusions. A survey conducted by the Commission for Racial Equality showed that young blacks only represented six per cent of the trainees on Mode A schemes in the public utilities — the schemes that involve work experience and have some chance of leading to a real job. Only 16 out of 1074 job opportunities in the two areas of the public sector surveyed went to black people. In the electrical and engineering groups surveyed only three out of 115 posts went to black youth (Commission for Racial Equality, *Employment Report*, October 1984).

Black people cannot rely on their trade unions to improve their position in the labour market. Too often union officials regard their black members with contempt and turn a blind eye to discrimination. A recent dispute at Reliance Cleaners, a large firm operating at Heathrow Airport, illustrates the complicity of the unions in racial discrimination. This firm has a long history of abusing its employees, particularly its Asian women workers.

In July Reliance announced the dismissal of its entire cleaning staff. To reduce its liability for redundancy payments, Reliance issued threats to some women staff, suspended some with five or six years' service for failing to clean properly and bullied others into resigning. The women were members of the Transport and General Workers' Union which promptly referred the matter to an industrial tribunal. The union's area representative, Jim McCloud, commented to a local reporter that 'if I know Indian people, they always have two jobs' and observed that 'if you offer nuts, you should expect monkeys'. Blaming the likely outcome of the tribunal findings on his members, McCloud complained that 'Asians are not willing to fight for themselves' (Southall Black Employment Unit statement). With union officials like McCloud it is not surprising that black workers have become cynical about the unions.

Not invincible

Unfortunately, Reliance — and McCloud — are not exceptional. This particular official may lack the subtlety of his superiors, but his attitude runs all the way from the smallest shop steward's office to the top corridors of the TUC. The racist consensus unites both sides of industry — at the expense of black workers.

Racism is as British as Lady Diana, the Houses of Parliament and the Union Jack. It is not an issue that raises eyebrows in polite society. Numerous surveys and investigations have detailed the day-to-day realities of racism in every sphere of British life. Even the Tory Home Secretary is prepared to admit the dimensions of the problem of racist violence. Every new study or media discussion only seems to confirm that nothing can be done about the problems of racial oppression. The fatalistic acceptance of the reality of racism has bred cynicism and despair. The prejudice that racism is natural and inevitable has acquired widespread currency. Many anti-racists lack the will to fight and simply go through the motions of doing something. Many black people have given up on the working class movement and look to their own communities to defend themselves.

The aim of this pamphlet is to argue that the triumph of British racism was not inevitable and that its current ascendancy is not unbreakable. Racism is not a product of nature but the result of social forces that have successfully walked all over their opponents. But racism can and must be fought. In the following pages we outline how British racism became such a powerful and pervasive force. Our aim is not merely to provide a historical record, but to throw light on the problems of the present. We explain the past failures and current paralysis of the anti-racist movement and outline a new approach to building an effective anti-racist movement in the British working class.

The ideas expressed in this book are based on the experiences of Workers Against Racism over the past four years. WAR groups in East London and elsewhere have shown that anti-racism does not have to mean pious platitudes and empty rhetoric, but can mean effective action.

1. What is racism?

Racism is too often discussed as something of a deviation from the norms of British political culture. It is also too often seen as a specific problem affecting the black immigrants of recent decades. To understand racism fully it is essential not to confuse racism as it exists today with the specific forms it has taken in British society in the past. Many observers tend to conflate the end result of the development of racism with its starting point. Racism has been a fact of life in Britain throughout the twentieth century. It has taken different forms and its force has been directed at a wide variety of victims. Before we look at the history of racism let's examine what racism really means.

Prejudice and racism

It is important to emphasise that modern racism is the product of modern capitalist society. Before the development of capitalism, concepts like racism, nationalism and chauvinism had no meaning. This is not to say that prejudices did not exist. In the old village-based communities prejudices were probably more diverse and more vicious than they are today. The small, socially homogeneous and self-sufficient villages of pre-capitalist Europe bred a strongly parochial outlook. People who spent most of their life in the village of their birth developed strong local identities. The harshness of life and the struggle to survive forced members of the community to rely on one another. Small-scale communal life also made people wary of outsiders, who were generally viewed with suspicion if not outright hostility.

In an environment where parochialism prevailed, superstition and prejudice were the inevitable response to the strange or unknown. The people of one region would acquire a reputation for being dishonest, another village would be labelled thrifty and people with special skills such as blacksmiths would be widely believed to have magical powers. With the passing of time, certain prejudices became fixed beliefs. When conflicts erupted these stereotypes shaped the way disputes were conducted among people from different villages or from different regions. The traditional rivalry between Lancashire and Yorkshire is one example of a conflict between groups of people with firmly held parochial prejudices. In pre-capitalist Europe fear of outsiders led to an attitude of suspicion against people who spoke a different dialect or language, worshipped in a different church or had a different colour skin.

At first sight many traditional prejudices appear to have a lot in common with modern racism. In both cases there is conflict between two different groups of people, in both cases hostility is based on irrational, and often fictitious, assumptions, and in both cases force may be used against the 'foreigner'. However, there is a fundamental difference between old-fashioned prejudice and racism. Parochialism is the typical fragmented response of isolated communities to outsiders. It is characterised by its restricted focus and rarely goes beyond the confines of a particular area. Because it is based on parochialism, prejudice is arbitrary and indiscriminate. Prejudices have no wider or longer term significance. To a Catholic peasant in a Lancashire village, a Protestant farmer from another region, a group of travelling tailors from Bradford, an African slave or a French visitor are all potentially equal objects of suspicion. His suspicions are most likely to be directed against the peasants in the next village who are attempting to gain more grazing rights from the lord's land at 'his expense'.

Traditional prejudice is an arbitrary response to the unknown with little social significance. Before the development of capitalism more general or national prejudices were very much the exception. The notion of pride in being British had little meaning to most people whose strong local identities overrode nationalist sentiments. Fighting for the nation against the French had little popular appeal. Soldiers either joined up for a share of the loot or in most cases declined the invitation and had to be forcibly conscripted.

Capitalism and racism

It is ironic that capitalism, which developed in the first place through a struggle against parochialism, later created the conditions for the emergence of racism. For the capitalist class, all parochial and regional barriers were an obstacle to development. Capitalism could thrive only by eliminating regional barriers and establishing a national economy and a national market. That is why the capitalists were the first consistent nationalists. In their historic struggle to eliminate parochial divisions and establish a nation-state, the early capitalists were a progressive force. Through this process they established a nationwide division of labour which created the framework for economic growth and technological development. The breakdown of parochialism widened people's horizons and made a positive contribution to social development.

The liberating role of the capitalist class did not last long. As soon as the capitalist economy was established, the ruling class became preoccupied with the necessity for maintaining its social power. The main instrument for the perpetuation of its power was the nation-state. In its struggle to secure its domination over society, the ruling class used the state to coerce the masses into carrying out the dictates of the capitalist system. For as long as the coercive character of the state was its most conspicuous characteristic, there was little popular support for the nation-state or for nationalism. In the early phase of capitalist development, British nationalism was widely seen as the philosophy of class exploitation and class domination.

In the late eighteenth and early nineteenth centuries, the British establishment had great difficulty rallying popular support for its 'national interest'. The ruling class was shocked by the popular enthusiasm for the French Revolution and the unpopularity of its wars against Napoleon. When the government's appeals to the nation fell on deaf ears it was forced to enact a series of repressive laws against popular movements and working class agitation. Repression at home was complemented by an aggressive foreign policy. Nationalism became less a weapon against parochialism and more an assertion of the will of British capital against its competitors abroad and its victims at home.

As the ruling class became more and more reactionary, the ideology of nationalism became more and more anti-foreign. The career of Thomas Carlyle illustrates this development. In his youth Carlyle was a passionate and courageous critic of British society. He was an articulate reformer in the best traditions of the early capitalist class. However, the European revolutions of 1848 made him rethink his position. This threat to capitalist stability made him acutely aware of the danger of the 'masses' to his class. He put his considerable talents as a publicist to use glorifying the 'English race' and justifying Britain's oppression of 'inferior people', who were appointed by God to serve.

Race as a social issue made its entrance with the establishment of the capitalist system. No sooner was the nation-state established than the progressive aspect of nationalism was discarded and it was transformed into an ideology to justify class domination and the oppression of foreign nations. Nationalism became overtly anti-foreign and racist for the first time. The racist tendencies within nationalism emerged most forcefully in the colonies. This was not due to any irrational prejudice. The intensity of racism against people of another skin reflected the intensity of their oppression.

The edifice of British racism was built on the foundations of the nation-state. It is important to note that racism first emerged as the outlook of the ruling class. It was not yet a popular sentiment in early nineteenth century Britain, but remained confined to the patriotic elite. In the 1820s, millions of ordinary people signed petitions demanding an end to slavery. Yet by the close of the nineteenth century racism had entered into the popular consciousness and had begun to influence significant sections of the working class. To understand this development we have to examine the relationship between racism and imperialism.

Imperialism and racism

The nation-state contributed decisively to the early development of capitalism. Yet as capitalist accumulation proceeded, national borders became a barrier in the quest for profits. The further development of capital required it to operate on an international scale. Capitalism entered its imperialist phase of development in the last two decades of the nineteenth century. Although capital became more international, the capitalist class became more dependent on its nation-state than ever before. There had been episodic conflict among the capitalist nations throughout the nineteenth century, but now capitalist competition was internationalised and every imperialist power was pitched into a relentless struggle for survival against its rivals. Imperialism led to the explosion of national differences.

Imperialism also led to a tremendous expansion of production. This expansion, fuelled by the plunder of colonies, generated vast wealth in the major imperialist powers, strengthening the position of the capitalist class. For the first time a proportion of capitalist profits could be spared to finance social reforms. Some of these super profits were also distributed to sections of the working class, creating a degree of class harmony and social consensus. Imperialism led to the emergence of a privileged layer of workers whose material interests were closely linked to imperialist expansion.

Higher living standards and social reforms helped to secure a consensus of support for imperialism. Nationalism ceased to be an elite ideology and became a mass force. Workers were prepared to identify the cause of the nation as their own because it seemed that their livelihoods, jobs and welfare depended on Britain staying ahead of its competitors. National survival came to be equated with success in routing foreign competition. It should be noted that the growth of nationalism was far from universal in Europe. In those countries where the capitalist class remained weak and ineffective in the competitive struggle, nationalism had only limited scope for growth. For example, the weakness of Italian capitalism, best illustrated by its defeat in Ethiopia in the late nineteenth century, prevented the establishment of a strong social base for nationalism.

The ascendancy of imperialism meant the oppression of the rest of the world. It meant the enslavement of the people of Africa, Asia, Latin America and the Middle East. The world became divided between oppressor and oppressed nations. A handful of imperialist nations oppressed most of the world. The ideology of nationalism legitimised imperialist oppression, the superiority of the coloniser and the inferiority of the colonised.

In the colonies, nationalism was not a matter of simple national rivalries. The imperialist powers asserted their right to colonise by treating the indigenous population as an inferior species. It was in the colonial situation that the vocabulary and culture of racism acquired a systematic form. In the imperialist countries racism entered the political culture but it lacked the immediacy of the colonial situation. Nor did it have any independent existence from the general chauvinist culture that prevailed in the imperialist nations. The United States, with its legacy of internal capitalist slavery and the presence of a sizeable black population, is an exception. In other imperialist countries racism only really emerged as an independent political force with the world-wide movement of labour in the twentieth century.

Immigration and racism

Capitalism created the working class and it continually reorganises it to perpetuate and enhance exploitation. The survival of capitalism depends on the reproduction of a class which owns nothing but its ability to work. Because the working class has no choice but to sell its labour-power it is dependent on capital. Capital dictates the terms on which labour is employed. As Marx argued, 'the labourer does not employ the means of production, but the means of production employ the labourer'(K Marx, *Capital,* volume 1).

Whether workers want to work or not is a matter of indifference to the ruling class. Jobs are provided not according to social need but according to the requirements of the capitalist system. When production expands rapidly, capitalism can provide relatively full employment and may even experience shortages of labour. Such periods are very much the exception. Most of the time a significant section of the working class remains without employment. In periods of economic recession millions are thrown out of work to increase the numbers of the unemployed — or what Marx called 'the reserve army of labour'. The reserve army is vital for capital. The existence of a pool of unemployed workers puts pressure on those in jobs to accept reduced wages and deteriorating working conditions. The reserve army weakens the working class as a whole.

The relationship between wage-labour and capital was modified during the imperialist phase of capitalism. As capital expanded into a world-wide system, the ruling class was no longer restricted to exploiting its own domestic working class. It could now employ and exploit workers in the nations that it oppressed. Moreover, in the colonies it could do away with the protections workers had secured in the West and impose more brutal conditions of exploitation. But imperialism was not content merely to enforce harsher conditions of exploitation in the colonies. The imperialist powers looked upon the colonial people as a mobile reserve army of labour that could be sent to any part of the globe according to their requirements. Chinese people were despatched to Hawaii and Malaysia, and Indians were sent to South and East Africa. A world-wide movement of labour was institutionalised as part of the imperialist system.

The migration of labour was not restricted to the colonial world. Workers were also imported from the colonies to be exploited in the imperialist nations themselves. Successive waves of immigrants to countries such as Britain, France and the United States have provided the capitalist class with a continuous source of cheap labour. Whenever the ruling class experiences a labour shortage or needs a specific type of labour it simply looks to the reserve army of labour in the oppressed nations.

Immigrant workers are not only useful but necessary for the imperialist system. The anarchy of the market means that sudden shortages of labour can arise in specific sectors at short notice. Sudden increases in the demand for labour can often only be met through the importation of workers. Immigrant workers are always in favour because they can be used to put pressure on indigenous workers. In the nineteenth century immigrant workers were sometimes used as scabs. Very often immigration is manipulated to prevent workers in employment from using their bargaining position due to the shortage of labour to demand better conditions and higher wages. Immigrant workers have always been particularly vulnerable to the dictates of capital. Even at the best of times, immigrants enjoy limited rights and are never allowed to forget their special status. Often the capitalist class can use them when it wants to and dispose of them when their services are no longer required. For the capitalist system this is one of the most attractive features of labour migration.

Labour migration from the colonies to the imperialist countries gave racism its immediate social and political significance in the West. Racism already existed within the imperialist countries as one aspect of a chauvinist culture. But it only became activated with direct social consequences once large-scale labour migration began. Immigration recreated important aspects of the colonial situation within the imperialist countries. The gulf between workers from advanced and backward capitalist countries was consolidated within the imperialist countries through a series of formal and informal measures which perpetuated the distinction between indigenous and foreign workers. This created the potential for divisive tensions within the working class, to the great advantage of the employers.

What is racism?

Racism is generally depicted as an attitude or a state of mind. This approach is misleading and can only lead to confusion. Racism is not an idea but a social force based on material conditions. Prejudice or superstitions about any group of people only become important in certain circumstances. Racist ideas have long existed in Britain, but the specific conditions of large-scale immigration that make racism an influential force in society are a very recent development.

The parallel between racism and anti-semitism helps to clarify the specific character of modern racism. Throughout its history Christianity has bred anti-semitic prejudices. Suspicion and dislike of Jews have characterised all phases of modern European history. But anti-semitism only acquired a social significance in areas of substantial Jewish population. Elsewhere anti-semitism was a part of the general culture but had little importance. It was a simple prejudice, with no more significance than the belief that the Earth was flat. Today, anti-semitism continues to have a resonance, but is of minimal social significance. Individual Jews may experience prejudice but only in an arbitrary and episodic manner. Whether or not anti-semitism becomes important in the future depends not on the idea of anti-semitism or the state of people's minds but on whether social conditions are recreated which galvanise anti-semitic prejudice against Jewish people.

It is the same with racism. The present day obsession with skin colour is a modern phenomenon and is not an essential ingredient or necessary condition for racism. In the past, all the discussion about race concerned the Jews and the Irish — in Central and Eastern Europe the Slavs were also thrown in. Today, these discussions are long forgotten and only the most backward people are preoccupied with these prejudices. In contrast, anti-black prejudices which used to obsess only the most decadent philistines have now become widespread. This is not because the ideas of racism have become intellectually more convincing but because social relations have changed.

We can now summarise the answer to the question — what is racism? The basis for racism lies in the capitalist nation-state. With the rise of capitalism and capitalist competition, nationalism acquired a virulent anti-foreign dimension. This ideology, which initially had a base of support limited to the capitalist class, became a part of mass culture in the era of imperialism. Since imperialism breeds oppression, nationalism was used to legitimise oppression. In the colonies it acquired a thoroughly racist form. Nationalism turned into racism in the relationship between oppressor and oppressed.

The extension of racism as a social and political force in the imperialist countries was effected through labour migration. This development came about, not through the importation of racist ideas, but through the establishment of the social structure of racism. From immigration controls to formal and informal colour bars, racist discrimination became a reality and racism acquired legitimacy. The inferior status conferred on immigrant workers perpetuates the division of the working class and provides the employers with a powerful weapon to dominate the proletariat as a whole. The acceptance of these divisions and the structure of discrimination creates a situation where racism becomes potentially an explosive force. Let's now look at how this potential was realised in the case of Britain.

2. Beneath the surface

The present structure of British racism is the result of a long period of historical development. We can identify four important phases in the growth of British racism. In the century leading up to the end of the Second World War, racism became established as an underlying current in British society. From 1945 to 1962, racism gathered momentum and became a part of popular consciousness. In the years from 1962 to 1979, racism became a real social force, backed by the state, political parties and labour movement organisations. In its latest phase, from 1979 onwards, racism has become an accepted part of the British way of life. Racism is now respectable.

The rapid expansion of the British Empire and the consequent increase in the national income fuelled a strident British chauvinism. During the last quarter of the nineteenth century chauvinist sentiments became widespread, influencing all sections of British society. However, the relative homogeneity of the indigenous population meant that this chauvinism did not assume a systematic racist character. British chauvinism was directed against the outside world, not against an enemy within. It was more a glorification of British imperialism than a response to issues of domestic concern. Racism existed as an underlying current and had little direct consequence. There were two important exceptions to this trend.

The first target of chauvinist outrage were the Irish. During periods of large-scale Irish immigration, anti-Irish feeling reached hysterical proportions. Despite the colour of their skin, Irish people were portrayed as a distinct and degenerate race. The popular press depicted Irish people not merely as inferior, but also as bestial and sub-human. Hostility towards the Irish was shaped by two important factors. Immigration had

'The Irish Frankenstein': the bestial Irish in *The Tomahawk,* 18 December 1869

brought to Britain the tensions of colonial Ireland. The intensity of the movement for Irish independence provoked a virulent chauvinist reaction within the British establishment. The second strand of anti-Irish sentiment stemmed from the insecurity of British workers who saw this large-scale labour migration as a threat to their way of life. This sentiment was not entirely irrational. British capitalists consciously used Irish immigrants to put pressure on the rest of the working class, to keep down wages and to keep militancy in check.

The immediate casualty of anti-Irish chauvinism was working class solidarity. The employers were able to use Irish immigration to divide workers and strengthen their hold over the whole working class. Marx was one of the first to draw attention to this development:

'The English bourgeoisie has not only exploited the Irish poverty to keep down the working class in England by forced immigration of poor Irishmen, but it has also divided the proletariat into two hostile camps. The English worker hates the Irish worker as a competitor who lowers wages and the standard of life. He feels national and religious antipathies for him. He regards him somewhat like the poor whites of the Southern states of North America regard their black slaves. This antagonism among the proletarians of England is artificially nourished and supported by the bourgeoisie. It knows that this scissor is the true secret of maintaining its power.' (Marx and Engels, *Ireland and the Irish question*)

The parallel that Marx drew between the attitude towards black people in America and Irish people in Britain was not an arbitrary one. The prevalence of racism cannot be explained by natural phenomena such as skin colour, but only by the social relationship of oppression. Oppression is the mainspring of the most decadent of racist stereotypes. Today, under different social conditions, Irish people rarely experience the traditional forms of racist abuse. It is easy to forget just how intense and widespread these sentiments were in the past. They were common even to Liberal and Labourist traditions. Sydney and Beatrice Webb, who exerted a powerful influence over the early Labour Party did not hide their contempt for the Irish:

'We will tell you about Ireland when we come back. The people are charming but we detest them, as we should the Hottentots, for their very virtues. Home Rule is an absolute necessity in order to depopulate the country of this detestable race.' (Cited in J Beveridge, *An epic of Claremarket*)

The Jews were the second group of nineteenth century immigrants to be singled out for special treatment. Since Jewish immigration was numerically less significant and more localised than the Irish influx, anti-semitism never reached the same pitch as anti-Irish chauvinism. But in certain areas like the East End of London, anti-Jewish feeling ran high. Led by the TUC, the official labour movement launched a campaign against cheap Jewish labour. Reactionary politicians joined in the chorus of abuse against the Jews, denouncing their alleged criminal behaviour and their tendency towards subversion, and warning of the threat that their diseases and unsanitary habits posed to the British nation. It was a sign of the times that the anti-Jewish agitation led eventually to the enactment of the 1905 Aliens Act, the first modern anti-immigrant law in Britain.

A turning point

The 1905 Aliens Act raises issues at the heart of the modern problem of racism. The most consistent campaigner against Jewish immigrants and the strongest advocate of immigration controls was the TUC. The anti-immigrant stance of the early trade union leaders has been a consistent theme in the history of the British labour movement to this day. It has led many people to conclude that the working class is the most racist section of society. Superficially, there is considerable evidence to support this view. Whereas the trade unions often see immigrants as a threat to jobs and living standards, the bosses look on them more favourably as cheap labour and a tool to divide the working class.

Trade union racism is a reaction to the instability created by the influx of immigrant workers into the labour market. It was this fear of competition for jobs that led the 1893 TUC conference to demand restrictions on immigration:

'In view of the injury done to a large number of trades and trade unions by the wholesale importation of foreign destitute paupers, this Congress calls upon the government to take the necessary steps, either by Bill, official inspection, or order in council, to prohibit the landing of all pauper aliens who have no visible means of subsistence.' (Trades Union Congress Report 1893)

Generations of union leaders have been repeating the same point, more or less diplomatically, ever since.

It is wrong, however, to identify the problem of racism as something peculiar to the working class. Indeed, it is the capitalist class which benefits from racism. As we noted in chapter 1, the capitalist class necessarily expresses its interests in the language of nationalism and racism. The establishment never talks in terms of its own class interests — it always presents its objectives as necessary for the good of the nation. Nationalism is a vital weapon for winning consensus at home and support for British imperialism abroad.

The growth of British nationalism in the latter part of the nineteenth century strengthened social stability and created a degree of class harmony. The acceptance of the view that workers had more in common with their British exploiters than with workers in other countries bolstered the position of the capitalist class. It meant that workers thought of themselves as British first and workers second. As a result, the proletariat could not act as an independent class. The growth of these sentiments in the labour movement meant that workers often came out with a nationalist response to political problems. As the number of immigrants increased, anti-foreign prejudices came into play and shaped the trade union response to instability in the labour market.

The capitalist class has a much more ambiguous response to labour migration. Far from feeling threatened, the employers view immigrants as workers who are particularly vulnerable to exploitation. The employers thrive on the divisions between immigrant and indigenous workers. Labour migration is more than welcome, it is essential for the capitalist class. However, the bosses cannot remain indifferent to anti-immigrant agitation. The ruling class cannot exhort the masses to be tolerant of foreigners, nor can it denounce nationalism. This would contradict its general emphasis on strengthening British nationalism. In other words, the ruling class cannot encourage nationalism in general and at the same time speak out against its particular manifestations.

The ruling class gives way to anti-immigrant sentiments because it appreciates the advantages of fostering nationalism in all sections of society. In any case, if it wants to exploit more immigrant workers it will always find a means to do so. Thus the 1905 Aliens Act did not close the doors to foreigners — its main purpose was ideological. The ruling class is aware that workers' economic insecurity and fear of labour immigration can be put to good use. It can be a weapon for limiting the influence of progressive tendencies in the labour movement. That is why ruling class policy combines short spells of unrestricted immigration with the mobilisation of anti-immigrant sentiments. The state has a keen awareness of the importance of racism for maintaining capitalist domination.

The significance of the 1905 Aliens Act now becomes clear. The anti-immigrant agitation turned worker against worker and it made British workers the spiritual slaves of their employers. The Act cost the employers nothing and in return they received the gratitude and goodwill of the TUC. Its long-term importance was considerable — it established a precedent for interfering in the movement of the working class and strengthened the conviction that there was a basic conflict between the interests of British and foreign workers.

Despite the considerable strength of chauvinism up to the Second World

War, race was not an issue in British politics. Racism existed behind the scenes, but it seldom intruded into public life. Racism only came to the fore in those rare instances when the indigenous population came into contact with the numerically insignificant black population. When this happened the result could be explosive even at this early stage in the development of British racism.

Racial tensions were rife in ports such as Liverpool and Cardiff which had visible black communities. In June 1919 these tensions exploded into a racial pogrom. Mobs of white thugs descended on the black residential areas, terrorising anybody in sight. *The Times* described the ugly scenes in Liverpool:

'White men appear determined to clear out blacks, who have been advised to stay indoors. This counsel many of them disregarded, and late on Sunday a large body of policemen had to be requisitioned to prevent serious consequences. Whenever a negro was seen he was chased and, if caught, severely beaten. These scenes continued until an early hour of this morning, when rain cleared the streets.' (11 July 1919)

Black people who fought back were arrested and jailed for assault and threatening behaviour.

Although black people were clearly the victims of white lynch mobs, they were held responsible for the pogroms. There was no question of solidarity with the black community. The *Liverpool Courier* was of the opinion that 'one of the chief reasons of popular anger behind the present disturbances lies in the fact that the average negro is nearer the animal than is the average white man' (cited in Peter Fryer, *Staying power*). *The Times* was no less disparaging. It disapproved of the 'intermarriage of black men and white women' which had 'excited much feelings' (10 July 1919).

The consensus view which blamed the victims of racism for their oppression also suggested a solution. When Liverpool's Lord Mayor met the chief constable and a labour ministry official on 12 July to discuss the race riots, their solution was to expel the blacks:

'It was decided that coloured men should be removed quickly from the Bridewell and other places in the city and placed in an internment camp pending repatriation, which will be expedited.' *(The Times,* 13 July 1919)

While the victims of racial oppression were being rounded up and deported the labour movement remained silent. The Labour Party ignored the racial aspect of the riots. In an article titled 'Race riots: the root cause', Labour's paper, the *Daily Herald,* called for immigration controls:

'Firemen and soldiers, who were specially concerned, had the gravest fear

as to the effect which the coloured influx was likely to have upon the rate of wages, and they said that unless checked in time it would spread to other industries and dominate the labour market.' (13 June 1919)

The *Daily Herald* portrayed foreign workers as a threat and turned economic arguments into apologies for racial violence.

The 1919 TUC conference did not waste its time with the now mandatory hypocritical resolutions denouncing racism. Delegates unanimously approved a motion making their position clear:

'That immediate steps be taken to abolish under-paid Asiatic labour in the mercantile marine, and that preference of employment be given, first to British white and secondly to British coloured, in preference to Chinamen.'

The events of 1919 showed that racism was potentially an explosive issue. But they were more a taste of what was to come much later than a prelude to an upsurge of racial violence. Britain did not become any more enlightened — all that happened was that racism remained a relatively unimportant part of popular culture. Even the fascist agitation against the Jews in the thirties had little resonance. British nationalists were more preoccupied with the threat from another foreign quarter — Germany.

Even during the Second World War, when large numbers of black people came to Britain to assist the war effort, racism maintained its low public profile. British nationalists concentrated their sights on their German rivals and welcomed help from any source — white, black or brown. But the widely held view that this was a period of racial harmony is a myth. While racism rarely took an overt form, an informal colour bar was in operation. A report detailing the position of black seamen in Cardiff showed that blacks were treated as second class citizens. Discrimination was widespread, especially in housing, and, despite their British nationality, blacks were classified as aliens (see Fryer).

During the Second World War the arrival of the racially segregated American army led to the extension of the colour bar into new areas. Certain restaurants, hotels and social clubs were declared out-of-bounds to black soldiers. These discriminatory practices never became an issue until the summer of 1943 when the famous West Indian cricketer Learie Constantine was turned out of the Imperial Hotel. Constantine's humiliation caused a sensation and a public outcry and he won his legal battle against the hotel. For every Constantine there were hundreds of West Indians who had to endure the humiliation of racial oppression in silence.

With the exception of the riots of 1919, race was not a political issue during the three decades that followed. Only civil servants and politicians around the colonial office kept the issue alive. They feared that it would have an adverse effect on the colonies if blacks in Britain mixed too freely with white people. This would give black immigrants ideas above their station and could turn them into trouble-makers when they returned home. These preoccupations had no long-term influence on the subsequent development of racism.

Lasting legacy

In this period racism became an unstated assumption of British life. Racist sentiments did not acquire a focus and had little political importance. But they were there, ready to emerge when the conditions were ripe. More importantly, racist assumptions were never confronted or challenged. As a result, even the more radical sections of society became part of the British chauvinist consensus. The Labour Party's firm commitment to British imperialism led it to adopt a patronising and chauvinist approach to the colonies. The party's 1933 report is typical:

'There are territories, for example, in the West Indies, where the people are probably already capable of managing their own affairs. There is no reason why they should not be given a large measure of self-government. On the other hand, the African territories, are in this respect, entirely different. Their people are in a condition which would make it impossible for them to take over the government of their country on modern lines. In such cases, what is required is education and preparation with the definite object of training the population in self-government.'(Labour Party policy report No 6, *The colonies,* August 1933)

The Labour Party was far from being the most racist of British political parties. But its attachment to the British Empire meant that it was incapable of challenging British chauvinism.

The main legacy of this period is the development of racism as an underlying current without the development of a current of anti-racism. The absence of an anti-racist tradition in the working class had serious implications for the future: it meant that the racists held the initiative and would always be in a position to establish the terms of discussion and debate.

3. Going public

From the Second World War up to the early sixties, racist views became much more popular. The underlying and often unconscious racist assumptions of the past took shape and became an established part of British public opinion. A number of important developments influenced this process. Large-scale immigration from the colonies in the post-war period provided a visible focus for the mobilisation of chauvinist and racist sentiments. The British state played a supervisory role, ensuring that immigration was identified as a problem and that racism became a coherent force. The establishment's successful pursuit of these objectives was more or less guaranteed by the full cooperation of the official labour movement and the lack of an anti-racist opposition.

The role of Labourism

Much has been written about the relationship between black immigration and the rise of racism. However, most commentators have accepted the link as direct and inevitable without attempting to unravel the connections. To make sense of this process it is essential to consider developments that have received little attention.

One of the least discussed but one of the most important factors that influenced the emergence of popular racism was the consolidation of chauvinism in the British labour movement in the forties and fifties. The Second World War enormously strengthened nationalism in the labour movement. Labour leaders were brought into the government and the trade unions were given important positions in the machinery of state in exchange for full cooperation in the war effort. The status accorded to the official labour movement during the war encouraged loyalty to the state.

Virtually every section of the working class fell under the spell of patriotism.

The growth of patriotism in the labour movement destroyed the last vestiges of anti-imperialist sentiment. A nationalist outlook was transmitted to large sections of the working class through the agency of the labour leaders. Even the left was influenced by pro-imperialist sentiments. *Tribune,* the leading paper of the Labour left, was not embarrassed about declaring its allegiance to British imperialism:

'We do not need to apologise for our mission in Africa. Whatever the reasons which took our forebears there we must stay.' (20 August 1948)

Keep Left, the manifesto of the Labour left, was equally forthright:

'Once we give up the attempt to hold the Middle East by force, we can concentrate our manpower and resources on the African development which should be our main colonial responsibility in the next thirty years....It is not an exaggeration to say that the failure of European socialism depends on the success of our combined colonial policies in the African continent.' *(Keep Left,* 1947)

The consolidation of nationalist and pro-imperialist views in the labour movement inevitably shaped its response to immigration. From the outset, the labour movement looked upon immigration as a danger. Some union leaders encouraged their members to oppose the employment of immigrants in their industry. The most vociferous opponents of immigration in the immediate post-war period were the unions influenced by the Communist Party. The response of the National Union of Mineworkers to the employment of Polish immigrants in the coalfields revealed the extent to which the unions had been corrupted by chauvinism. Led by its Communist Party General Secretary, Arthur Horner, the NUM launched a vigorous anti-Polish campaign.

Horner did not mince words. He warned the government that 'Britain depended for its coal upon the goodwill of the miners and if anything was done to defeat the purpose of the miners then they might get Poles or displaced persons but not coal' *(The Times,* 24 February 1947). Horner's outburst set the tone for every trade union leader's response to the arrival of immigrant workers. It was proof that pro-imperialist sentiments in the labour movement provided a fertile terrain on which racism could thrive.

The consequences of this chauvinist approach soon became apparent. In August 1948, the agitation of the National Union of Seamen to prevent the employment of black seamen on British ships provoked a race riot. A year later, white racists in Deptford set upon newly arrived black immigrants. Local Labour politicians were quick to pin the blame on the black victims.

Labour MP John Lewis took the matter up in Parliament and demanded an immediate statement from the Labour government's under-secretary of state on the Deptford events. He got one:

'I am informed that towards midnight on 18 July, some coloured men began to shout abuse to passers by from a window of a common lodging house...a large crowd gathered and there was some disorder. The police...were assaulted and obstructed by these coloured men.'

Councillor Sherwood of Deptford council put the local authority's view:

'The recent disturbances were unfortunate but the fault was not all on one side. From time to time coloured people come here...and we have got to do something with them. They are happy-go-lucky people who come here to what they regard as the land of the free. They look for a job and whether they like it or not there are some people who do not want to work with coloured folk.' *(Kentish Mercury,* July 1949)

The Deptford incident showed that Labour had become an apologist for racism. It would be wrong to portray the leaders of the labour movement as the most racist section of British society in the forties. But by virtue of their special position of authority over the working class, the labour leaders shaped the popular response to immigration. They rarely made explicitly racist statements — that was left to the Tories. But by presenting immigration as a problem, they ensured that the response to black people more often than not assumed a racist form.

'A necessary evil'

After the Second World War British capitalism was faced with an acute shortage of labour. The establishment operated an open door immigration policy and actively encouraged black workers to come to Britain. Although the British government was keen to recruit immigrant labour, the authorities wanted to ensure that immigrants lived and worked on their terms. Hence the government set out to create a category of second class citizens to complement its policy of unrestricted immigration. The discussions between civil servants and the post-war Labour government codified the ruling class approach to immigration.

From the start, the Labour government presented black immigration as a necessary evil. Home Secretary J Chuter-Ede told a meeting of the Cabinet Foreign Labour Committee in 1946 that 'he would be much happier if the intake could be limited to entrants from the Western countries, whose traditions and social background were more nearly equal to our own and in whose case it would be possible to apply the sanctions of deportation' (Minutes, 14 March 1946). Minister of Labour George Isaacs made the same point in response to the arrival of West Indian immigrants on the *Empire Windrush* in 1948:

'I hope no encouragement is given to others to follow their example.' *(Hansard,* 8 June 1948).

Isaacs was to be disappointed; immigrants were essential for capitalist recovery and there was no alternative but to put up with them.

In public the Labour government continued to peddle its 'necessary evil' line. In private it began to devise ways of enforcing the inferior social position of immigrants. Minister of Health and hero of the Labour left Aneurin Bevan typified this approach. At every meeting of the Cabinet Foreign Labour Committee, Bevan pleaded for more immigrants to be deployed in the newly established National Health Service. At the same time, he insisted that the needs of British workers must come first. He argued against building houses for immigrant workers in the coalfields on the grounds that it 'would reduce still further the already low standards of amenity of many mining areas and create bad feeling about the foreign workers who would be put in them' (Minutes, 26 February 1947).

The 1949 anti-black riots confirmed the Labour Cabinet's view that black immigration meant trouble. Its immediate response was to tighten government control over the black population. The Cabinet discussion concluded that racial tension was highest 'in areas where there is substantial general unemployment and in establishments where white workers are employed'. However, the Labour leaders blamed blacks for the trouble:

'The principal obstacle...is the attitude of some of the coloured colonials themselves and their undisciplined behaviour.'

To instil some imperial discipline the Cabinet recommended 'a policy of dispersal of unemployed colonials to other areas' (Cabinet Minutes, cited in *the next step,* March 1981).

The Labour government began to explore ways of keeping black people out of Britain by imposing some form of immigration controls. On 19 June 1950, the Cabinet appointed a committee of ministers to 'arrange for a review to be made of the further means which might be adopted to check the immigration into the country of coloured people from the British colonial territories' (Cabinet Papers, 1951). In February 1951, the committee reported its findings to the government. It reviewed different options for controlling immigration and concluded that it wasn't worth the effort given the small number of black immigrants involved. But the Cabinet had accepted the legitimacy of racial discrimination and warned

'A necessary evil': the post-war Labour government gave immigrant workers a cold welcome

that controls might be necessary in the future:

'We are aware, however, that in the long term, social standards in the colonies lower than those in the United Kingdom may well result in considerable migration to this country, and that the social services in the UK, particularly the rights of which any destitute person can avail himself under the National Assistance Act, must inevitably act as considerable attraction. We recognise that a very large increase in such migration in the future might produce a situation in the UK rendering legislation for its control essential, despite the very strong opposing considerations which we have mentioned.' (Cabinet Papers, 1951)

In the fifties British capitalism did not need immigration controls. The Labour leaders recognised that it would be counter-productive to go public and enshrine state racism in legislation. Instead, the Labour government worked behind the scenes, planning out a strategy for the time when immigrants were no longer vital for the economy. In the meantime it allowed informal colour bars to spread into virtually every sphere of social life. The Cabinet allowed racial discrimination to flourish and put every obstacle in the way of those who tried to combat it. This was evident in the Cabinet's response to the attempt by Labour MP Reginald Sorenson to pass a Private Member's Bill in Parliament 'to make illegal any discrimination to the detriment of any person on the basis of colour or race'.

Chuter Ede spoke for the Cabinet when he declared in April 1951 that 'the subject is one which might prove embarrassing for government supporters in Parliament'. The Bill itself was hardly radical. It ignored discrimination in housing and employment, the areas where the colour bar operated with the most devastating effect. Nevertheless, the subject of the colour bar was taboo to the Cabinet. It decided not to oppose the Bill in public, but to manoeuvre behind the scenes to block it. The Cabinet sub-committee dealing with the legislation concluded that 'the Bill should not be blocked at the present stage, though this would be necessary later' (Cabinet Legislation Committee meeting, 3 April 1951). Another blow was struck for the colour bar.

By the time it was removed from office in 1951, Labour had established the basic framework for state policy on immigration. These policies were still at an early stage. The time for a fully-fledged system of state discrimination had not yet arrived. Informal colour bars were sufficient to isolate immigrant workers and divide the working class.

The incoming Tory government merely carried on where Labour left off. A bipartisan policy, which rejected the need for immigration controls in public while planning them in private, was established. There is a widespread view that successive governments in the fifties fought a valiant rearguard action against racist prejudices. In reality, both Labour and Tory governments popularised the notion that immigration was a problem and encouraged the spread of an informal colour bar. Prime Minister Winston Churchill summed up the attitude of the British establishment when he argued that Jamaican immigration would make Britain 'a magpie society: that would never do' (cited in Zig Layton Henry, *The politics of race in Britain).*

Out of the closet

Racist propaganda and anti-immigrant campaigns began almost as soon as the first black workers stepped ashore in Britain. A great deal has been written about the racist activities of right-wing Tories in the late forties and early fifties. Reactionaries like Cyril Osborne, Conservative MP for Louth, conducted a vocal anti-black campaign in Parliament. But racism could not have become a major political issue merely as a result of the work of a handful of Tory backbenchers. That required a more complex process in which the official labour movement played a crucial part.

From the moment they landed, black immigrants faced discrimination in housing, social services, employment and in hotels, pubs and clubs. Black workers quickly discovered that they were wanted for one thing and one thing only — to work in jobs which white workers were not prepared to perform. As one company manager explained:

'We began employing coloured workers in 1956. You couldn't get a good white worker unless you were prepared to pay over the odds, and good coloured people are better than bad white people. You can't get good white people to do the menial tasks that have to be done in any foundry not even floating workers like the Irish.' (Cited in P Wright, *The coloured worker in British industry)*

Black immigrants also faced discrimination when they were not at work. The chauvinist tradition of the labour movement meant that immigrants were often greeted with suspicion by their workmates. In the conditions that prevailed in post-war Britain this suspicion soon turned into fear. The welfare state was more a promise than a reality and bad housing and social services were the norm in British cities. Urban decay became even more visible with the arrival of a distinct group of immigrants.

The new black ghettos were the product of widespread discrimination in housing. Treated as unwelcome guests, black workers had no claim to council housing. They were forced into rented slums in which overcrowding in decaying dwellings became the norm. An investigation by the Economist Intelligence Unit revealed that 54 per cent of Coventry's immigrants lived in single room accommodation in the first year after arrival.

The new immigrants' slums that dotted the urban landscape and the isolation imposed on black people through colour bars heightened the sense of difference between white and black. Politicians were not slow to blame black people for the housing shortage and inadequate welfare services. Blacks themselves were held responsible for the inferior housing conditions in which they were forced to live. The victims of discrimination were made the scapegoats for the failures of the welfare state.

Instead of fighting for better housing and services, Labour politicians pointed the finger at foreign workers. They claimed that the influx of black immigrants was a drain on scarce resources. It became commonplace for Labour politicians to complain that the Tory government was dumping immigrants in areas already facing major problems. Anti-Tory rhetoric of this sort inevitably bred resentment against the immigrant community. It also gave legitimacy to the arguments of the more racist sections of British society. There was little scope for the right to cash in on the race issue when local Labour Parties were making blacks the culprits for every social problem. In 1955 the Labour-controlled council in Lambeth complained of the burden that West Indians were placing on housing facilities. Lambeth council had little sympathy for the plight of black families. As far as the Labour Party was concerned, any improvement in housing provision for black people could only be made at the expense of 'the people of Lambeth'. Local Labour leader Martha Marack stated clearly that white people came first:

'Coloured families, even though some are living in miserable conditions, will get no more housing priority than ordinary Lambeth people. If we put the immigrants into council property, then it must be to the detriment of the people of Lambeth who have been waiting for houses for many years.' *(South London Press,* 28 January 1955)

The Labour Party's approach was to cast immigrants as competitors for scarce jobs, houses and services. Black people were blamed not only for their own appalling conditions, but also for the problems confronting the local community. In 1954 and 1955, Brixton's Labour MP Marcus Lipton led a series of delegations to Whitehall demanding that the government relieve the burden of immigration on Lambeth and surrounding areas. Lipton personified Labour's hypocritical approach to the immigration question. He loudly condemned racism and discrimination, while bemoaning the problems that immigration had caused in his constituency.

Labour politicians rarely made openly racist speeches. Indeed, the 1956 Labour Party conference passed a motion denouncing racial discrimination. But while it condemned racism in one breath, the Labour Party encouraged it in another by equating immigration with social problems. The significance of this approach became clear in November 1957, when five Labour MPs in London — Albert Evans (Islington South), Eric Fletcher (Islington East), BJ Parker (Paddington North), W Gibson (Clapham) and Marcus Lipton (Brixton) — demanded a parliamentary debate on housing and immigration. These Labour politicians went to great lengths to establish their anti-racist credentials. But the debate which they initiated only reinforced the view that immigrants were the cause of the housing problem. A growing number of MPs were now seriously considering pushing for some form of immigration control.

Instead of challenging racist prejudices, the official labour movement encouraged the popular belief that immigration was a problem that had to be checked. This approach was not explicitly racist — indeed, it often involved attacks on Tory policies and demands for better housing and services. But the consequence of Marcus Lipton's argument that the housing problem in London was growing 'because it is bound to grow so long as immigration into this country continues...it is bound to grow so long as building by local authorities is restricted' was to focus attention on immigration and not on the lack of housing provided by the system.

Despite its public repudiations of the evils of racism, the official labour movement promulgated the view that immigration was the cause of many of the social ills facing the working class. This had a decisive influence on the development of modern British racism. By legitimising the idea that immigrants were a problem, the labour leaders allowed more systematic racist views to gain a hearing among wide sections of British society. The chauvinist assumptions that underpinned their approach paved the way for a convergence between Labourism and the more coherent racism of the right. Right-wing politicians could prey on the fears of working class people and channel them in an explicitly racist direction. Although they did not often manifest themselves in public, racist ideas gathered momentum. When race riots exploded in London and Nottingham in 1958, however, it was no longer possible to pretend that racism was not an issue.

The eruption of racial violence in Nottingham and Notting Hill in the summer of 1958 exposed the xenophobic sentiments that now gripped sections of British society. Labour and Tory spokesmen united to blame blacks for bringing the attacks on themselves. This response went hand in hand with claims that these were exceptional events and that racism was alien to the British way of life. British capitalism still needed immigrant labour; its faithful servants in the Tory and Labour Parties were not yet ready to make race the focus of political controversy.

On the streets, however, racism made its presence felt. The 1958 riots showed that popular prejudice against immigrants was now a fact of life. Politicians of all the main political parties took note of this development and accommodated to it. The commonplace view that some politicians fought a battle against the racist prejudices generated by ordinary people is specious. At best, some Labour politicians made moralistic appeals for racial harmony and avoided confronting racism head on. This was the approach of Labour Party leader Hugh Gaitskell. However, his vaguely anti-racist rhetoric was never directed against those who took a less enlightened view of the matter in his party.

Other politicians fought to be the first to stand up for the rights of British workers. North Kensington Labour MP George Rogers claimed to speak for his constituents in Notting Hill when he attacked local blacks for their failure to adapt to the British way of life:

'The main cause is...housing...people living in overcrowded conditions. To add to the difficulties some West Indians make no effort to adapt themselves to the way of life here. Whilst thoroughly condemning the riots and violence, naturally there is resentment that West Indians can buy homes here.' *(Kensington News,* 5 September 1958)

Nottingham Labour MP James Harrison saw the anti-black riots as a compelling argument for restricting immigration. In areas of high immigration local Labour Parties took their cue from Rogers and Harrison. The local Labour establishment in Coventry gave 'very serious consideration to the recent disturbances involving coloured and white people in other parts of the country'. It was worried about the 'potential difficulties that the five thousand coloured people in Coventry might cause' and proposed an inquiry (*Coventry Evening Telegraph,* 5 September 1958).

Race and politics

The official response to the 1958 race riots was a boost to the racists. Local racist pressure groups, such as the Immigration Control Association in Birmingham, were established in a number of cities. At a national level a growing number of MPs were demanding controls on immigration from the Commonwealth.

Throughout the fifties racism developed as a local issue. The ruling class was happy to present immigration as a problem and to divide the working class by perpetuating the colour bar. But it recognised the disadvantages of turning race into a national issue at a time when British capitalism desperately needed a supply of foreign labour. The establishment had no need of legislation; it could rely on the informal colour bar, local politicians and the police to enforce the conditions of racial oppression.

In the late fifties the ruling class changed its approach towards the question of immigration controls. This shift in policy was not simply a response to local pressure. The changing requirements of the capitalist system provided the real impetus for a new strategy. By the late fifties the first signs of crisis made their mark on the British economy. Unemployment rose in 1957 and unskilled workers were no longer at a premium. The sharp rise in black unemployment during the short-lived slump of 1957 was a sign of the times (see Ministry of Labour and National Service Report, 1957). For the capitalist class the importation of immigrant labour was no longer such a pressing necessity.

The second factor impelling the ruling class to adopt a new approach to immigration was political. For years the establishment had fostered the growth of British chauvinism. Now it could no longer afford to ignore its more popular expressions. The Tories also grasped that an immigration clampdown could have considerable electoral appeal and help distract attention from their unusually poor performance in government. Enoch Powell personified this shift in policy. In the fifties, Powell was all for immigration. He played an important part in recruiting immigrant labour from the West Indies. His subsequent career as the ideologue of British racism is well known. His conversion was not the result of a personality crisis, but an expression of the influences that began to prevail in ruling class circles from the late fifties onwards. The 1962 Commonwealth Immigration Act was the fruit of these developments.

The 1962 Act made the state directly responsible for enforcing racial oppression. Race took its place at the centre of the national political arena and became a major topic of debate. Informal colour bars were superseded by systematic discrimination in every aspect of social life. Race was no longer a local affair, but a national issue. Prejudices once whispered behind closed doors were now forcefully articulated for public consumption.

Race was transformed into a political issue in the fifties with scarcely any opposition. There was no such thing as an anti-racist movement. A few black militants spoke out, but they spoke out alone. Anti-racists proclaimed the brotherhood of man and left it at that. They railed against bad housing, but avoided confronting racism directly. The left, such as it was, saw racism as an affliction peculiar to right-wing Tories or simply pretended that it did not exist. Racism went from strength to strength, not because its opponents were vanquished, but because it had no real opponents.

4. As British as the Union Jack

In the sixties and seventies racism became a legitimate topic of discussion and a major force in British society. It was no longer the clandestine property of a minority, but an everyday reality sustained by statutes and laws. Racism was no longer simply a component of popular consciousness. It had become a burning issue and one capable of mobilising significant numbers. Increasingly, it became one of the most useful weapons for consolidating the power of the capitalist class.

The establishment set about elevating racism from a local into a national issue. Now that the economy no longer needed new supplies of immigrant labour the Tories had no qualms about establishing themselves as the anti-immigrant party. It was now possible to reap the maximum benefits of the divisive effects of racism. In the past immigrants had been a necessary evil; now they were no longer even necessary. This was the substance of the message from the ruling class.

Like all immigration controls, the 1962 Commonwealth Immigration Act endowed racism with respectability. It activated latent fears about the threat posed by immigration and encouraged committed racists to take things even further. The media and other establishment institutions promoted the intrusion of race into all walks of political life. The lack of any serious resistance to this process was both a symptom of the climate of uncertainty and an indication of the collapse of the liberal opposition.

This collapse was most evident in the case of the Labour Party. Out of office the Labour leadership took a hard line against the Tories' 1962 Act. A year later, however, when it came to discuss its commitment to repeal the Act, Labour prevaricated and then capitulated. Party leader Harold Wilson's admission that 'we do not contest the need for immigration controls' said it all *(Hansard,* 27 November 1968).

Once Labour had accepted the need for immigration controls the racists had all the cards stacked on their side. Minor incidents were magnified into events of national importance. The arrival of Asians expelled from East Africa in 1968 became the subject of a debate that raged and raged. In 1972, the arrival of 27 000 Ugandan Asians was a cause for national outrage. In 1976, four Malawi Asian families who were given temporary accommodation in a four star hotel were pilloried in the national media. Any immigrant receiving anything anywhere was hunted down and held up as another national humiliation by the hacks of Fleet Street.

Race did not become a national issue spontaneously. The British state made it one by establishing a national framework of discrimination. The 1962 Immigration Act was only the first in a series of racist laws. Under successive Tory and Labour governments new immigration laws increased the scope of legal discrimination. Other agencies of the state — from the police, to the judiciary, to the welfare state — followed suit. Parliament and the courts had defined immigration as a problem. This meant that any form of racial discrimination could receive the sanction of the law.

Leprosy is infectious

Even today millions of white Britons describe themselves as non-racist. In the sixties large sections of British society rejected the racist label. How then did racism become such a significant social force and immigration such a burning issue?

The overwhelming influence of British nationalism provided the foundation for the growth of racism. Nationalism, even in its more innocuous forms, emphasises the centrality of Britishness. It is by its very nature exclusive. Immigrants are automatically dismissed as 'different', 'foreign', 'outsiders'. The anti-immigrant lobby simply activated these sentiments by inflating the 'immigrant threat'. In times of uncertainty, and especially in times of economic crisis, these xenophobic arguments are even more appealing. Thus in every debate on immigration the more sober British nationalists have always yielded to the more aggressive racists.

The right has successfully used the issue of race to put pressure on the left. In particular, the right has taken advantage of Labour's incoherence on the issue to influence the Labour Party electorate. Labour's defeat in its former stronghold of Smethwick during the 1964 General Election is a good example. The Tory candidate Peter Griffiths, dubbed a 'parliamentary leper' by Harold Wilson, played the racist card for all it was worth in his successful campaign to oust the sitting Labour MP Patrick Gordon Walker. The Smethwick campaign illustrates the evolution of the Labour Party's policy on race.

Right-wing local politicians had been whipping up racial prejudice in Smethwick for some time before the election. Despite his benign reputation, Labour's Patrick Walker was hardly a friend of the immigrant community. Back in 1954 he had joined a number of Labour MPs in calling for immigration controls. His response to the introduction of a 'whites only' rule by a Smethwick landlord evaded the issue:

'I can see nothing to be gained by changing the well-established law of this country which leaves the question of licensing to the local licensing justices.'(Cited in Miles & Phizacklea, *White man's country)*

Even this masterly display of equivocation did not spare Walker from the wrath of the Tory racists.

Walker is often portrayed as a dignified victim of the right and a fervent anti-racist. Nothing could be furthur from the truth. At different times, Walker chose either to ignore the growth of racism or to adapt to it. Rather than fight the racists he paraded his nationalist credentials. Under pressure from the racists in 1962, Walker sought to reassure his constituents:

'This is a British country with British standards of behaviour. The British must come first.' (Cited in Paul Foot, *Immigration and race in British politics)*

Walker dug his own grave. If the British came first then the racists' argument that immigrants had to come second made perfect sense.

Walker changed his tack during the election campaign. He tried to outflank his opponents by blaming the Tories for letting immigrants into Britain. He took to criticising his opponents for being part-time racists. A leaflet put out by the Labour Party just before the election illustrated this cringing approach:

'Be fair: immigrants only arrived in Smethwick in large numbers during the last 10 years — while the Tory government was in power. You can't blame Labour or Gordon Walker for that. Labour favours continued control of immigration, strict health checks and deportations of those convicted of criminal offences.' (Cited in Foot)

Walker found himself vying with his Tory opponent to attack the black community. But even this gross capitulation to the racists did not spare him from the humiliation of electoral defeat.

The racists did not confine their activities to Smethwick. They hammered the Labour Party at Perry Bar in Birmingham and at Eton and Slough. In Southall the Labour majority was reduced to 1897 and the British National Party candidate scooped 3410 votes. Under pressure from the racists, the Labour Party did on a national scale what Walker had done in Smethwick — it made concessions. Within a matter of months leading figures in the Labour Party underwent a conversion. Roy Hattersley's gift for adapting his principles to suit the times was a product of this period. Up to 1964 Hattersley was a 'passionate' defender of free immigration. In 1965 he won the applause of Tory backbenchers when he admitted his mistake:

'Looking back on the original Act which limited the entry of Commonwealth citizens into this country I feel that the Labour Party of that time should have supported it....I make this point with no great joy because I was a passionate opponent of the Act.' (*Hansard,* 24 March 1965)

The new Labour government did not simply drop its opposition to the 1962 Immigration Act. It set about establishing a more comprehensive system of controls. In August 1965 its White Paper *Immigration from the Commonwealth* strengthened controls on an explicitly racist basis. Cabinet minister Richard Crossman made no apologies for Labour's surrender to the racists:

'This has been one of the most difficult and unpleasant jobs the government has had to do. We have become illiberal and lowered the quotas at a time when we have an acute shortage of labour....Nevertheless I am convinced that if we hadn't done this we would have been faced with certain electoral defeat in the West Midlands and the South East. Politically fear of immigration is the most powerful undertow today.' (R Crossman, *Diaries of a Cabinet Minister,* volume 1)

With the passing of time the job became less 'difficult'. Labour's tough line on immigration paid dividends in the 1966 General Election.

The Labour Party demonstrated its capitulation to the racists in its response to the 1968 'Kenyan Asian crisis'. The influx of British Asians from Kenya provoked an hysterical anti-immigration campaign by Tory right wingers. At the height of the debate the Labour government panicked. It introduced a Bill removing the right of entry of black UK passport holders. The Bill passed through all its stages in record time — three days — to become the Commonwealth Immigrants Act (1968). Labour politicians cited the Act as proof of their commitment to halt the alien invasion. In East London, Stepney MP Peter Shore tried to offset criticisms from local racists by proclaiming Labour's anti-immigrant credentials:

'I understand the anxieties that you and some of your workmates have expressed about the flow of immigrants. The fact that they tend to concentrate heavily in a small number of already densely populated areas inevitably increases the housing and social problems that already exist.

'This was, of course, one of the main reasons why the Labour government decided to cut back the number of immigrants. Last year only 5000 work vouchers were issued — a very big reduction from the 30 000 or so that were being issued as recently as 1963. If the total rate of immigration still remains high, it is not due to the present government voucher policy but to the arrival of dependants of those immigrants who came here in the fifties and early sixties. Only a few weeks ago, the Commonwealth Immigrants Act further tightened up controls and, in particular, strengthened the law against illegal entry.'

The Labour leaders viewed their concessions to the anti-immigrant lobby as a necessary expedient. Having demonstrated their pro-British credentials, they hoped that the right would be satisfied. Crossman's reflections on his visit to Smethwick in 1970 expressed this complacency:

'Racialism has been extremely violent in this area but there were many more questions about doctors and nurses and secondary schools. There is no doubt that stopping immigration, which was one of Callaghan's great achievements, has done an enormous lot for us and that in places like Smethwick the racial undertone, which was enormously strong in 1964, is now weaker than in 1968.' (Crossman, *Diaries*).

Crossman was proved wrong. Racism did not disappear — indeed the anti-immigrant stance of his party contributed to its growth.

Throughout the seventies the ruling class continued to play the racist card. The Tories stepped up their anti-immigrant offensive and implemented the 1971 Immigration Act which closed the doors even more tightly than before.

In the mid-seventies, right-wing racist parties, notably the National Front, gained votes and wider influence. The right-wing climate took its toll on the 1974–1979 Labour governments. The Wilson-Callaghan regime tightened up immigration controls and introduced barbaric virginity tests for Asian brides arriving in Britain. In 1977 it produced a Green Paper whose proposals were later implemented in the Tories' 1981 Nationality Act.

By the 1979 General Election, racism had become so much a part of the policies of the main political parties that far-right groups like the National Front were redundant. Who needed the National Front when establishment leaders like Margaret Thatcher were flaunting their racist credentials?

'The British character has done so much for democracy, for law, and done so much throughout the world that if there is any fear that it might be swamped, then people are going to be rather hostile to those coming in.' (*The Guardian*, 31 January 1978)

The Labour Party was indignant — not at Thatcher's broadside against the black community, but at the suggestion that it had failed to do its bit to keep Britain British. Home Secretary Merlyn Rees denied that Labour was 'soft' on immigration. 'The exclusion figures speak for themselves', he boasted in 1977, 'over 1100 deportations were made and nearly 500 illegal immigrants removed' *(The Times,* 16 February 1978).

Peter Griffiths, the 'parliamentary leper' of 1964, would have felt quite at home inside the ruling circles of the Tory and Labour parties of 1979. A bipartisan policy on immigration had been established. Individual Labour politicians had reservations on the subject, but under pressure from the right they felt disinclined to press the point too strongly.

The enemy within

Immigration controls are designed to keep a grip on immigrant workers. They provide the legal framework for controlling the migration of workers into Britain and the life of immigrants inside Britain. The legal distinction between Britons and non-Britons is the basis for two different types of citizenship. Immigration controls define a section of society as second class citizens and legitimise their oppression. In the latter half of the seventies the ruling class had already achieved its objective of stopping the flow of primary immigrants. It now set about hounding the black community in Britain.

The police have always paid special attention to the black community. Even before immigration controls were introduced, the police enforced the informal colour bar. There was no law against racial discrimination and, as far as the police were concerned, everybody was entitled to practice whatever prejudice they pleased against the black community. For the police, immigrants were 'different' and therefore potential trouble-makers. They needed to be kept in their place.

At an early stage police began to churn out their now familiar justification for terrorising the black community. Because of their 'culture', so the argument went, blacks had no respect for authority and they tended to be out of work because they were 'lazy'. This is how one Police Chief Inspector justified a raid on a West Indian house in Brixton where men were found playing cards at the height of the 1957-58 recession:

'When police find a house of this description every endeavour must be made to suppress it. The majority of men are not working. Many have never worked while they have lived in this country and have money from various means.' (Cited in *Race Today,* May/June 1980)

Raids continued throughout the sixties. Brixton police station became notorious for its 'nigger hunting' expeditions. In 1962 local police raided a West Indian home in Mostyn Road, claiming that alcohol was being sold on the premises. The defendants managed to convince the magistrate that they were enjoying a family party at the time of the raid. The Mostyn Road defendants were lucky. The majority of poilce raids went unreported and hundreds of families had to endure the indignity of police repression in silence.

Racial oppression inevitably provoked resistance and inflamed relations between the police and the black community. The police response was swift and ruthless. Any attempt to organise resistance met with the full force of state repression. In 1969 a black activist was jailed for nine months for distributing 'inflamatory leaflets':

'Scotland Yard is keeping a watchful eye on the black power situation in Brixton and areas with immigrant concentrations where the movement is gaining strength because they fear that trouble could escalate within a few years.' *(South London Press,* 13 January 1970)

In the sixties, police attacks on the black community were sporadic. In the seventies, the shift from external to internal control resulted in a more systematic campaign of police repression.

Black and blue: police terror became a fact of life for black youth in the seventies

Thousands of victims of police repression remain anonymous. But a number of publicised incidents in the seventies indicate the conscious, coordinated role of the police in enforcing racial oppression. During the summer of 1970 the police unleashed a wave of terror against the black community in Britain's inner cities. The large-scale harassment of black youth and multiple arrests under the notorious 'sus' law, led to clashes in the streets of London. On 9 August, the police reacted by attacking a demonstration protesting at the threatened closure of the Mangrove restaurant in Notting Hill. Nine black militants were charged with riot and assault. The case of the Mangrove 9 was only the first in a series of show trials designed to criminalise black resistance. The police provoked similar confrontations at the Brockwell Park festival in 1973, at the Carib Club in 1974 and in Chapeltown in 1975. In 1976 tensions exploded in a prolonged battle at the Notting Hill carnival.

Police repression was backed by a propaganda campaign. Up to the seventies the focus of racist hysteria was the threat of immigration to the British way of life. Once primary immigration had ceased the focus shifted to the threat to the social fabric from the 'foreigners within'. Immigrants were no longer just an undefined 'problem'; they were now denounced as criminals. In 1972, 'muggers' became the synonym for black youth. At key

This way out Mrs Begum: the deportation toll mounted from the seventies onwards

moments throughout the seventies the police released bogus statistics to prove that black criminals represented a threat to the British way of life. Academics commissioned by the Home Office came to the same conclusion. A report published in 1979 noted that West Indians had a 'propensity to engage in crime' *(The Guardian,* 4 December 1979).

Criminalisation became a central component of state racism. By labelling blacks as criminals, the state could justify stepping up police attacks on the black community. 'Saturation policing' became a euphemism for police invasions of black inner-city ghettos. The occupation of Brixton by the Special Patrol Group in the closing weeks of 1978 was one illustration of the new approach. Patrolling the area in armoured cars, squads of armed police conducted on the spot searches and interrogations:

'The Brixton operation involved 150 officers, 120 SPG men and 30 detectives from Scotland Yard. During the month they made 430 arrests and charges and questioned 1000 people.' *(South London Press,* 8 December 1978)

After terrorising black youth in Brixton, the SPG moved on to Hackney in East London to brutalise the black community there.

Criminalisation justified increased police repression against the black community. It also encouraged racists to take more direct action against blacks on the streets. The police offensive coincided with an upsurge in racist violence. Racial attacks on black people predate this period. In May 1959, a West Indian carpenter Kelso Cochane was murdered by a gang of white thugs. But from the early seventies racially motivated attacks assumed a new dimension. 'Paki-bashing' was the new racist sport; by 1970 it had become a national phenomenon. In areas like Tower Hamlets and Newham in East London, the Asian community lived in a state of perpetual terror. Local politicians and the media buried their heads in the sand and tried to pretend that the problem did not exist. On 4 May 1978 Altab Ali was stabbed to death by a gang of racists in East London. Thousands of local people took to the streets in protest. A month later Ishaque Ali was murdered in the same way in Hackney. This time 19 000 Bangladeshi workers came out on strike. It was no longer possible to ignore the mounting tide of racist violence. Racist attacks had become an everyday reality.

Racist violence on the streets is the unacceptable face of British racism. Every establishment figure and party politician feels compelled to condemn it. But racist attacks did not spring from nowhere. They are the result of the long build-up of racial tension during which the leading institutions of the British state established a legal framework of discrimination. The judiciary and the law have legitimised racism. And a system of police repression exists to enforce it. When racism becomes respectable, racist attacks are inevitable.

On the defensive

The explosion of racist violence in the seventies did not go entirely unchallenged. From Bristol to Brixton, black youth fought back against the police and the racists. After decades of ignoring racism, the left finally began to take an interest in the issue. Left-wing newspapers had occasionally carried articles condemning racism, but these had no practical consequences. The main impulse behind the growth of an anti-racist movement was the rise of the far right. In the mid-seventies the fascists began to make inroads into the Labour Party's electoral base. It was fear at this threat to the official labour movement rather than a sense of solidarity with black workers that spurred the left into action. In June 1976 an internal report on the growing electoral menace of the National Front compelled the Labour Party to take a stand against fascist violence. At the TUC conference the same year, the union leaders went out of their way to denounce racism and the National Front.

It is significant that the leaders of the labour movement were moved into action by an instinct for survival rather than by a desire to defend the black community. Their response was not so much anti-racist as anti-fascist. Indeed, in this period the terms anti-racist and anti-Nazi were used interchangeably. Anti-fascist activity became popular on the left, reaching its apogee with the formation of the Anti-Nazi League in 1977.

The National Front provided the left with a convenient diversion from the task of fighting racism. The Anti-Nazi League was an opportunist attempt to cash in on the widespread anti-fascist sentiment that prevails in Britain. Anti-Nazism is not the same thing as anti-racism. It is possible to be a British nationalist and an anti-Nazi and a racist. The left's anti-fascist activity was directed not against state racism, but against its unacceptable face. Leading Socialist Workers' Party member and Anti-Nazi League supporter Alex Callinicos was forced to concede that 'paradoxically, at a time when the growth of the Anti-Nazi League has isolated the Nazis, their radical ideas are more influential than ever before' *(Socialist Review,* May 1978).

The irrelevance of the Anti-Nazi League to the anti-racist struggle became clear after the 1979 General Election. National secretary Paul Holborrow announced that it was being wound up because the National Front's electoral threat had receded:

'We were formed to deal with the prospect of a massive Nazi intervention in

the General Election. Since then the Front has deteriorated into schisms. We don't want to cry wolf and artificially jack up something that is not as strong as it was two years ago.' *(Time Out,* 2 May 1980)

The left's aggressive attacks on the National Front stood in sharp contrast to its defensive approach to the issue of racism. The left simply avoided the question of immigration controls. At its June 1978 conference, the Anti-Nazi League decided that opposition to immigration controls was not binding on its members. Meanwhile, the Communist Party and the Labour left argued that Britain needed non-racist immigration controls! The left's inability to take a consistent stand against all immigration controls was reflected in its whole approach.

Instead of meeting the racists head on, the left argued that immigrants were not as big a problem as they were made out to be. It tried to reassure the public that immigrants were good for the economy. Even the far left echoed this defensive approach. Every time the racists attacked black people the left sought refuge in economic statistics. The Socialist Workers' Party argued that the racists had got their figures wrong. At the height of a virulent anti-immigrant campaign in 1978, it observed that 'in fact, immigrants are a benefit to the economy'. The SWP's apologetic tone only underlined the inefficacy of its argument:

'Many black people will feel that it is insulting and degrading to them even for socialists to argue about the immigration and birth rate figures in the way we have done. Why shouldn't black people enter the country freely and have as many children as they want? It is, nonetheless important to let people have the facts on the issue. (Socialist Workers' Party, *The case against immigration controls,* 1978)

Not only were these arguments degrading, they were also ineffective. Racism cannot be fought with 'facts'. What if immigrants had a higher birth rate than the indigenous population? Would socialists then support immigration controls?

The limited scope of the anti-racist movement in the seventies undermined the potential for developing the arguments necessary to take on the racists in Parliament and on the streets. The left was in retreat from the start and made concession after concession to popular prejudice. As a result, the establishment was able to manipulate racial divisions to its advantage with very little opposition.

5. Riding the storm

For many people the post-1979 period is an enigma. In the 1979 General Election the Tories stood on a forthright racist platform. They kept their promises and proceeded to implement the most far-reaching of racist laws, the 1981 Nationality Act. In the summer of 1981 riots flared in every inner city and shook the establishment to its foundations. Two years later things had changed dramatically. Race was not a major issue in the 1983 General Election. The Tories even made a play for the black vote with their slogan 'Labour says he's black, Tories say he's British'. To make sense of these developments we have to examine the two-pronged strategy pursued by the ruling class.

The strong-arm state

During the first three years of the Thatcher administration the state stepped up its offensive against the black community. The Tories reduced immigration to an all-time low. The government introduced new immigration rules in March 1980 which prevented large numbers of immigrants from joining their families in Britain. Deportation orders shot up from 1275 in 1979 to 2472 in 1980. The 1981 Nationality Act, which came into force in January 1983, extended the scope of immigration controls and allowed the state to systematise its internal surveillance of the black community.

The Nationality Act marked the end of an era of immigration regulation and the start of a crackdown on the settled immigrant population. Even before the Nationality Act came into effect, the establishment had taken steps to extend racial discrimination into new spheres. In October 1981 the Department of Health and Social Security launched a 'feasibility study', checking patients' 'ethnic origins', in 10 hospitals. The aim of the pilot project was to test out the response before introducing hospital charges for overseas visitors. The DHSS also called into question the right of immigrant workers to receive supplementary benefits. In February 1982 'ethnic monitoring' was launched in 14 unemployment benefit offices, ostensibly for statistical purposes.

The purpose of the new vogue for ethnic monitoring in the public sector was to establish a category of second class citizens. These would be identified primarily by skin colour and subjected to tight internal controls. In 1981 and 1982 the immigration authorities carried out a series of factory raids — 'fishing expeditions' — in search of 'illegal immigrants' as part of their new role as the state's immigration policemen. The implementation of the Nationality Act in January 1983 heightened fears of an internal clampdown. That month the police launched a series of passport raids in London — more than 30 homes were raided. Similar attacks occurred in the Midlands. The Immigration Service Intelligence Unit established a new computer with files on hundreds of thousands of people to assist state control. All this was intended to create a climate of fear and terrorise the black community as a whole. Immigration controls are inherently racist — they call into question the rights of every immigrant. They make every black person a potential 'illegal'. Police raids are a constant reminder to the black community of its inferior status in British society.

During 1983, Home Office collaboration with the DHSS was established on a regular basis. Black people are now expected to produce passports to prove their immigration status when registering with a family doctor, attending hospital, signing on for social security or unemployment benefit, getting on the housing waiting list, or enrolling at school or college. Even the most mundane aspects of everyday life have become a trial for black people. In October 1983 a newspaper report revealed that it was customary in many parts of the country for black people to produce passports when applying for marriage licenses. It was only after considerable publicity that the left-wing Labour council in Camden apologised to an Asian woman who was asked for her passport before being issued with a marriage license.

Police repression and the criminalisation of black people were overriding factors in the state offensive. Police harassment of black youth was so intense during Thatcher's first two years in office that the uprisings of 1981 had long been predicted. Police repression set off the chain events which began with the disturbances in Brixton in April 1981. In a major operation, appropriately called 'Swamp 81', nearly 1000 people were stopped and 118 were arrested. This was the spark which lit the flames of rebellion a few days later.

The 1981 events provided the excuse for tooling up the police. Newly equipped mobile riot police — Instant Response Units — were introduced in London. In March 1982, the establishment launched a major anti-mugging campaign to justify increased repression against blacks. The police played an active role. In October 1982 deputy chair of the Police Federation, Inspector Basil Griffiths, outlined the police response to the riots at a Monday Club meeting at the Tory Party conference:

'There is in our inner cities a very large minority of people who are not fit for salvage....The only way in which the police can protect society is quite simply by harassing these people and frightening them so they are afraid to commit crimes.' *(The Times,* 7 October 1982).

Another representative of the Police Federation expanded on the same theme a few weeks later:

'There are two conflicting demands. One is to stop harassing young blacks in the inner cities. The other is to stop young blacks harassing other people in the inner cities. Which demand do you respond to? It has to be the second.' *(The Guardian,* 20 November 1982)

The law and order campaign provided the backdrop for the publication of the Police and Criminal Evidence Bill in November 1981. In many ways the Bill merely legitimised prevailing police practice. Many of the repressive measures it proposed had long been in operation on the streets of Britain's black inner-city ghettos. Nevertheless, the codification of these powers in law was an indication of future trends. The appointment of Sir Kenneth Newman, the former head of the Royal Ulster Constabulary in Northern Ireland, as Metropolitan Police commissioner in October 1982 signalled that the lessons learned on the streets of Belfast would soon be brought to bear on the black ghettos.

Newman pursued a more selective form of counter-insurgency. Twenty-four mobile patrols involving 500 riot police toured the streets of London ready to be deployed with speed and efficiency. Looking back on the 'quiet' summer of 1984, Newman boasted of the success of the establishment's post-riot strategy:

'During the summer this year there were many mini-riots which had the potential to escalate to Brixton 1981 proportions. But they were quickly and effectively extinguished. So effectively, indeed, that they hardly rated a mention in the press.' *(The Guardian,* 17 October 1984)

To understand why the state has been so effective in containing black resistance, we need to look at the other side of its approach.

The response of the British state to the 1981 riots was twofold. With one hand it dished out repression, with the other a government grant. At the same time as it was rearming the police with plastic bullets, CS gas, riot gear and water cannons, the establishment was launching a sophisticated campaign of containment. Containment represents the soft side of the state's post-riot strategy. But it is no less deadly than coercion — it co-opts and corrupts potential opponents of state racism and isolates the victims of racial oppression. The race relations industry came into its own in the aftermath of the 1981 riots — but it has a long and sordid history.

Keeping the lid on

The anti-black riots in Notting Hill and Nottingham in the late fifties, and the spectre of large-scale riots as in the USA in the sixties, encouraged successive governments to sponsor a number of bodies to absorb black unrest. Labour governments were particularly sensitive to the need to contain the anger and frustration of the oppressed. The Race Relations Board, set up by the Wilson government in February 1966, typified all such institutions. Despite all the publicity and all its promises, the Race Relations Board did nothing to fight racial discrimination. It conducted many investigations and published a host of reports and did nothing. In its six years of existence, the Board took up 2987 cases, but only 7 got as far as the courts.

When the recession made repression more intense and revolt more probable, the Labour government passed the Race Relations Act in 1976. This Act incorporated earlier state race relations organisations into a central Commission for Racial Equality and numerous local Community Relations Councils. The Commission brought together government functionaries, middle class blacks and labour bureaucrats. Its first chairman was old Etonian and former Tory MP David Lane. With his experience as Minister for Immigration at the Home Office from 1972 to 1974 and adviser to the Association of Chief Police Officers from 1975 to 1976, Lane was ideally qualified for service in a quango designed to mop up the mess caused by state enforced racism. The trade union leaders had their own reasons for participating: they feared that growing competition in the labour market could upset stable industrial relations. Engineering union leader Bill Simpson, one of the first union officials to join the race relations industry, voiced the anxieties of the trade union bureaucrats:

'Britain could be the scene of militancy among immigrants within 10 years unless race relations in industry improve.' (Cited in Monty Meith, *Brothers to all men?*)

The record of the Commission for Racial Equality is just as abysmal as that of its predecessors. From its first investigation in 1977, the CRE has embarked on nearly 50 cases — 14 have been dropped and 19 are still to be published. The average investigation takes five years. Not surprisingly, an official inquiry into the CRE in the wake of the 1981 riots found that much of its work was irrelevant to the needs of the black community. Critics of the CRE have pointed out that it is ineffective. But the race relations industry was never meant to be effective. It is inconceivable that the state which doles out racial oppression day in and day out could pursue anti-racist investigations with vigour. The job of the race relations industry is containment. It has been most effective in this role in the years since the 1981 inner-city revolts.

After 1981 the ruling class recognised that it needed a more effective means of dampening black resistance. The establishment was well aware that it could not provide the jobs, houses and amenities that black people needed. As *The Times* commented cynically on the appointment of George Young as Minister for Race Relations in 1981:

'One is reminded of the Soviet Minister for (unobtainable) Fruit and Vegetables.' (12 February 1982)

The Thatcher government overcame its aversion to quangos and state hand-outs and despatched Michael Heseltine to improve race relations in Liverpool. The Tories were keen to integrate a layer of middle class blacks to help isolate the militants in the black community. Young outlined this approach:

'It helps if there are more black councillors, JPs, solicitors, accountants and other professionals. It is happening now, slightly faster with the Asian community than with the West Indians. It's not the whole answer of course. The middle class will never absorb two million people. We've got to back the good guys, the sensible, moderate, responsible leaders of ethnic groups. If they are seen to deliver, to get financial support from central government for urban projects, then that reinforces their standing and credibility in the community. If they don't deliver people will turn to the militants.' *(The Sunday Times,* 10 October 1982)

The Tories had some success in cultivating the black middle class, but they had a limited capacity for integrating black militancy. That was a job for the Labour Party. After the 1981 riots, the Labour Party — especially in left-wing Labour councils — moved into the sphere of race relations in an even bigger way than before. Backed by the Tory government's £270m Inner City Partnership funds, managed by the Department of the Environment and distributed through local authorities, the race relations industry mushroomed at a local level.

The most ambitious experiment took off in London, where the Greater London Council gave the race relations industry a new lease of life. By 1984 it was distributing grants to more than 200 community groups and had staked its claim to be London's leading anti-racist fighter. In fact, the GLC's approach was consistent with the Tory government's strategy. An informal division of labour was established. As *The Guardian* commented:

'There is very little that the GLC is doing which could be said to fall outside the recommendations of the Joint Government/Local Authority Association Working Party report.' (30 May 1984)

In the three years from 1981 to 1984 the race relations industry boomed. With full backing from the state, Labour councils launched 'equal opportunities programmes', set up new race relations committees and provided funds for a host of community projects. Tory councils followed suit: Bradford demonstrated that it too could play the GLC game.

The revamped race relations industry has worked wonders for the British establishment. Following the American model developed after the race riots of the sixties, the British version sought to co-opt and corrupt potential leaders of the black community. Local black defence committees were given funds and access to resources. In many cases they were successfully integrated into the apparatus of the local state. Hundreds of grants were dispensed in East London, Brixton, Handsworth, Liverpool 8, Chapeltown and elsewhere from the coffers of local and central government. For every instance of police harassment, racial violence and state oppression, Labour councils provided a committee or an adviser or a community project through which protest could be safely channelled and black anger quickly dissipated. Police committees and police monitoring groups proliferated and served to defuse resistance to the police and neutralise the anger of the oppressed. In Lambeth these policies were so successful that in 1982 the local Labour council and the police were able to move in and bulldoze the 'Front Line' of Railton Road with the acquiescence of 'community leaders'.

Labour councils played an invaluable role in keeping the black ghettos under firm control. A West Midlands Labour councillor proudly defended his council's radical policy of funding community projects, claiming that it had been 'overwhelmingly successful in defusing the tension which created the street riots of 1981' *(The Guardian,* 1 February 1983). The British establishment agreed. In September 1983, the editor of *The Times* insisted that the community approach should continue while the riot police were kept on full alert:

'The fact that we have had two summers free from inner-city rioting should

Softly, softly: co-optation and containment for black youth in Handsworth

Tooling up: the iron fist for Brixton's black rioters

not be allowed to justify any dilution in the government's commitment to an inner-city policy which was forced upon it by the events in Brixton, Toxteth and Moss Side.'

The success of the state's containment strategy was evident during Lord Scarman's return journey to Brixton in September 1984. Three years on from his inquiry into the causes of the unrest in Brixton, Scarman went back for a second look. Not surprisingly, things had got worse. Unemployment had doubled and as Scarman was forced to concede:

'Racial disadvantage is still perceived as the lot of young black people.'

But three summers had gone by without any riots and Scarman sang the praises of the radical race relations industry.

At an acceptable level

Racial oppression intensified under the Thatcher regime. The recession made the subordinate position of black people worse. The 1981 riots indicated the determination of the black community to fight for its dignity and rights. The British ruling class noted this, and to its armoury of repression it added the more subtle strategy of containment. During the subsequent three years this two-pronged approach worked with devastating effect.

Co-option and containment are part of the new technique of racial domination in the eighties. The British establishment is fighting hard to cope with the problems of social and economic instability thrown up by the recession. It can do without further street revolts by angry black youth. The ruling class wants to pursue a form of racial domination that will not provoke resistance. That's why, despite her unwavering hostility to immigration and her continued commitment to the criminalisation of black youth, Thatcher did not play the racist card in the 1983 General Election.

The British establishment is full of self-confidence about its present policies on race. The ruling class has no inhibitions about voicing its racist views in public. The Tories were not shamed into stopping the publication of the Policy Studies Institute's exposure of the Metropolitan Police in November 1983. The PSI report revealed that racist attitudes and language were 'expected, accepted and fashionable' in the police. Metropolitan Police commissioner Sir Kenneth Newman dodged the issue by arguing that the police were prepared to put their own house in order. The media chose not to pursue the point.

The PSI survey of the Metropolitan Police was not the only report to draw attention to the deep-seated racism of British society. In 1984 another PSI publication, *Black and white Britain,* documented the pervasive character of institutionalised racism. In June 1984, the *Employment Gazette* confirmed that racial discrimination was a major contributory factor in the high rates of black unemployment. A month later, the CRE's 1983 *Annual Report* admitted that racism was rampant:

'The level of racial discrimination in Britain remains high. It's manifestations range from outright physical attack, which in some parts of our cities remains depressingly prevalent, to systematic discrimination in areas of employment, housing and services.' (CRE, *Annual Report 1983)*

Racism is no longer a matter of public controversy — it has become accepted as a fact of life. Even racist violence has become acceptable. During the summer of 1984 revelations about the high level of racist violence against Asians in East London were duly acknowledged by the media and then quickly forgotten. As the casualties of racist terror have continued to mount, the British establishment has simply raised the threshold of what it considers to be an acceptable level of violence.

The Tories have managed to make racism acceptable, not only because they call the shots, but because they have a monopoly on much of the race relations industry. This is what makes the British establishment so confident. Since 1981 the combined efforts of the CRE, the Manpower Services Commission and local government have led to the institutionalisation of anti-racism. This is a remarkable achievement. The same state which legitimises and enforces racial oppression has been able to neutralise and incorporate the anti-racist movement. The hundreds of law centres, community projects, youth clubs, police monitoring groups and other parastatal organisations that sprang up in the wake of the 1981 riots testify to the considerable adaptability of the British state machine.

Many black activists and white anti-racists were not blind to the dangers of immersing themselves in the race relations industry. The radical director of the Institute of Race Relations, A Sivanandan, combined an appeal for blacks to work with the GLC with a warning about corruption:

'Don't let's be purists and stand outside, for we can't fight the system bare-handed. We don't have the tools, brothers and sisters; we've got to get the tools from the system itself and hope that in the process five out of ten of us don't become corrupt. If we've got to get the tools and Ken Livingstone's GLC is prepared to give them, we should not hesitate to use them.' (A Sivanandan, 'Challenging racism: strategies for the 80s', *Race and Class,* autumn 1983)

Sivanandan's 'five out of ten' has turned out to be a wildly optimistic estimate.

The neutralisation and corruption of many activists in the race relations industry is not the result of personal failings. Involvement in the soft arm of the state breeds an outlook which eschews struggle. It domesticates dissidence, neutralises opposition and pre-empts trouble. The radical race relations industry provides an in-house service for dealing with the debris of police repression. After the police have done their job, the quango activists move in to clean up the mess and heal the wounds. The institutionalisation of the anti-racist movement confirms the old Marxist dictum that the capitalist state cannot be used for progressive ends. Every radical activist employed by a Labour council is performing a sterling service for the British ruling class.

The British ruling class has achieved a remarkable feat in containing black unrest at a time of intensifying racial oppression. This was made possible by the retreat of its political opponents. The Thatcher government has faced no coherent challenge to its racist onslaught. The 1981 riots could have provided a unique opportunity to turn the tables on the establishment racists. But the left was so steeped in the tradition of British law and order that it sought to distance itself from the violence of the oppressed. It preferred to talk about anything — unemployment, social deprivation and 'over-policing' — rather than the issue at stake. In contrast, the ruling class seized the propaganda initiative and went on the offensive against 'black muggers and criminals'. The left capitulated, ensuring that the debate was not about racism, but about policing, law and order and black criminality.

By the time the British Nationality Act was implemented in January 1983, the left had abandoned the field of battle. The British state was so confident that it could promote itself as the champion of anti-racism. It ratified the CRE's *Code of Practice* for combatting racial discrimination in employment. This meant nothing and cost nothing, but the government escaped without criticism. The Tories were content to let their Labour opponents pursue harmless campaigns against Robertson jam 'golliwogs' and other soft targets. The institutionalisation of the anti-racist movement is the most significant development in the post-1979 period. It has helped to stabilise relations between oppressor and oppressed and to mould a new consensus in favour of state racism.

6. Divide and rule

One of the themes that recurs throughout the history of British racism is the irrelevance of the anti-racist movement. At crucial junctures it has barely existed; in other periods it has proved ineffective. Before we can change this situation we need to explain what has gone wrong in the unions and on the left over the past four decades.

A trade union can be an important weapon in the fight against racism. Here and there it is possible to discover examples of white trade unionists standing up for their fellow black workers. In September 1972 a group of building workers in Birmingham broke up a demonstration called to protest at the arrival of Ugandan Asians. More recently, in 1984, workers at British Leyland's Longbridge plant struck in protest at the victimisation of black worker Zak Mills. Unfortunately, these examples of working class solidarity are few and far between. The trade union movement has been complicit in perpetuating racist practices and institutions. The TUC was a staunch advocate of immigration controls in the early years of this century and held up the 1905 Aliens Act as a victory for the labour movement.

In the post-war period the trade union leaders were at best suspicious of black workers and at worst vocal in their opposition to immigration. In 1955 the TUC General Council told the Minister of Labour that since the government was responsible for maintaining full employment, it should ensure that immigration was controlled. A year later, the National Union of Railwaymen joined the chorus demanding restrictions on entry. This demand met with little opposition from the leaders of the TUC. At its 1957 conference, the Transport and General Workers' Union declared that it could not afford to allow 'these people unrestricted access to Britain' because it 'would lead to a reduction in the union's industrial bargaining power' *(TGWU Record,* August 1957).

In the fifties and sixties the trade union bureaucracy did not disguise its hostility towards immigrant workers. In some cases the union leaders went out of their way to make an issue of immigrant labour. The National Union of Seamen was constantly bemoaning the 'problem' of foreign seamen. Its journal regularly published letters calling for 'a ban on foreign nationals' and demanding 'British ships for British seamen' *(The Seaman,* July 1974). The TUC's Hotel and Catering Committee took a similar view. It declared war on 'illegal immigrants' and argued that 'the police, the Immigration Service Intelligence Unit and other authorities should be afforded substantially more resources to trace overstayers and to tackle all aspects of illegal immigration'. The committee endorsed any measures necessary to realise this objective:

'It was therefore agreed to inform the Home Secretary that his proposal for using the National Insurance scheme to identify those workers who need authority to work was worthy of further consideration, and that more resources should be provided to improve enforcement.' (TUC Hotel and Catering Industry Committee, Minutes, 19 July 1978)

The anti-immigrant stance of the union bureaucracy was not restricted to a handful of right wingers. In 1979 the Communist Party-dominated Furniture, Timber and Allied Trade Union was found guilty of colluding with employers at a Birmingham factory to discriminate against Asian employees *(The Guardian,* 5 May 1979).

From the top

It is widely accepted that the trade union leadership's attitude towards immigration is simply a response to rank and file pressure. According to this thesis, the union leaders are forced to adopt anti-immigrant policies against their better judgement. Many union leaders use this argument to justify racist practices and to shift the blame on to their members. In reality, it is the trade union bureaucracy which fosters chauvinist and racist sentiments among rank and file workers.

When it came to racial prejudice the union leaders were way ahead of public opinion. Many years before racism acquired a popular resonance, they were vigorously condemning the influx of foreign workers. Shortly after the Second World War, the National Union of Mineworkers pretended that there was no such thing as a labour shortage and campaigned against the employment of Polish immigrants. In 1947, the Communist Party-controlled Civil Service Clerical Association, the forerunner of today's CPSA, barred Poles from membership of the union (Annual Report, 1947). At its conference the same year, the union passed a resolution condemning the employment of Poles in the civil service. The Communist Party gave full backing to its supporters among the leaders of the miners and civil servants:

'I ask you, does it make sense that we allow 500 000 of our best young people to put their names down for emigration abroad, when at the same time we employ Poles who ought to be back in their country and bring to work in Britain displaced persons who ought to be sent back to their own countries.' (Harry Pollit, *Looking ahead,* 1947)

The campaign against Polish immigrants got a lot of publicity but failed to strike a chord with the public. During a Cabinet discussion on immigration Aneurin Bevan noted that the main enemies of the Poles were the 'communist elements' in the unions (CAB 134/341, 26 September 1946).

The trade union response to Polish immigrants anticipated the welcome accorded to black workers in the future. Throughout the next decade trade union leaders appealed to successive governments to impose stricter rules on immigration. The trade union bureaucracy's anti-immigrant campaign did not, however, reflect a groundswell of anti-foreign opinion. In the fifties, most workers were indifferent about immigration. Why then did the trade union bureaucrats take such a hostile stand against immigrant workers?

Workers form trade unions to defend their interests against the employers. Trade union officials are elected by rank and file union members to represent them in negotiations with the bosses. However, as the unions grow in size there is a tendency for officials to develop an outlook distinct from that of the rank and file. A recent survey of British trade unionism explains this phenomenon:

'Rank and file workers are interested in unions as organisations that fight for better wages and conditions. When they come into conflict with employers they turn to the unions to help them pursue their struggle to victory. Trade union officers must respond directly to the demands and pressures of rank and file members. But they also face additional pressures. As a union builds up a national structure it acquires office premises, full-time administrative staff, office and printing equipment. It also amasses a quantity of funds to cope with all sorts of expenses. Hence while union officials take heed of workers' demands, they also have to take responsibility for preserving the union machine — and their own position within it.' (Mike Freeman, *Taking Control,* 1984)

The development and expansion of British unions was paralleled by a growing divergence between the interests of the union leaders and the interests of the rank and file. The union leaders increasingly came to see every dispute as a potential threat to the union machine. Prolonged strikes were a drain on resources and disrupted the smooth running of union institutions. As far as the union leaders were concerned, it was far preferable to rely on laws passed by Parliament rather than the class struggle to pursue workers' objectives. The TUC came to see state intervention as the best guarantee of improving working class living standards.

The rise of the labour bureaucracy was consolidated through the growing involvement of union leaders in the state machine. The establishment conferred special privileges and status on the union leaders in return for keeping their members in check. During the late thirties and the Second World War, the ruling class took this process one stage further and directly involved the union leaders in the running of the state. This was the period when trade unionism became respectable and collaboration between union leaders and management became institutionalised:

'The long and painful transition from the barricades to the boardrooms has at length been accomplished, and today the TUC exerts its influence not so much through strikes and demonstrations, as through reasoned arguments before an independent arbitrator or an industrial court — or in the Cabinet Room.' *(The Times,* 2 November 1946)

The result was that the TUC became inextricably tied to the British state, with important consequences for trade union policy. Trade union leaders developed a firm commitment to the British nation and in particular identified their interests as trade unionists with the success of 'their' industry in its competitive struggles abroad. This did not stop trade union leaders from fighting for their members. It simply meant that they identified their members' interests with those of their employers. This accounts for the chauvinism that is such a marked characteristic of the TUC. Indeed, trade union leaders sometimes appear more chauvinist than any other section of society. As the TUC's nationalist rhetoric gained ascendancy, the language of the class struggle virtually disappeared.

One of the main concerns of union leaders is to ensure the stability of the labour market. For union leaders, the unemployed or any influx of new workers into the labour market is seen as a potential threat. While British trade union leaders have long been loyal to the national interest, they have remained staunchly sectional in their determination to defend the privileges of union members against unorganised sections of the working class. Trade union organisation has been directed not only against employers, but against competitors for jobs from outside the ranks of the unions. Thus union leaders have generally been hostile to the unemployed, to women workers and to immigrants, because they threaten the stability of the labour market.

Trade union hostility to unorganised workers was particularly fierce in the decade following the Second World War. In these years the trade union leaders enjoyed unprecedented national status. In return for their moderation and cooperation in rebuilding the post-war economy, the union leaders were drawn into the corridors of power. The TUC rejoiced in its high prestige, as transport workers' leader Arthur Deakin told Congress in 1952:

'It is notable that both the Prime Minister, Mr Winston Churchill, and the leader to the Labour Opposition, Mr Clement Attlee, testified publicly to the statesmanship shown by the leadership of the trade union movement, and the clear understanding by the Congress as a whole of the real needs of the nation.' (TUC Report, 1952)

The TUC was very pleased with itself. But its prestige depended on its ability to hold down the working class and force workers to make sacrifices in the interests of their employers. The TUC could get away with this because it could point to the fact that mass unemployment had been abolished. As long as virtually everybody had a job the TUC could appear to be effective to workers and continue to play its 'statesmanlike' role on the national stage.

The union bureaucracy was hostile to immigration because it feared that a large-scale influx of workers would upset the stability of the labour market on which its new found prestige depended. Union leaders saw immigrants as a threat to the carefully created arrangements that allowed them to take the credit for full employment. The chauvinist prejudices of the labour bureaucracy predisposed it to look upon immigrant workers as outsiders to the labour movement.

Although the union leaders had a material interest in opposing immigration, rank and file workers did not. However, in the absence of any alternative, the ideas of the union leadership gained a strong grip over the working class. In previous decades British nationalism was established as a legitimate point of view, even on the left wing of the workers' movement. Nationalist sentiments could easily be turned into a racist response to immigrants. In a movement in which even left-wing union leaders proudly paraded their war medals and gave patriotic speeches, prejudice against foreign immigrants easily gained a hold. Workers could still hold up banners proclaiming 'unity is strength' because this slogan could be interpreted to mean the unity of British workers against 'cheap labour' from abroad. By the early fifties racial discrimination was endemic in working practices in industry and services. The trade union bureaucracy bore a heavy responsibility for allowing this state of affairs to develop.

Shopfloor racism

Workplace discrimination has been the experience of immigrant workers from the beginning. It began because employers hired immigrant workers to do jobs that indigenous workers would not accept. Regardless of education or skill, immigrant workers were employed to work in conditions which British workers had already rejected. Employers were pleased to discover that they had the full backing of the trade unions in treating black workers in this way. Indeed, the trade unions went a step further and demanded that immigrants be placed in positions where they could not compete with British workers.

Even in the fifties when there was still a shortage of labour, the unions began to organise against the employment of black workers in skilled and supervisory jobs. Invariably the issue of competition for jobs acquired a racial dimension and extended from the union offices down to workplace level. In the Midlands, for example, the unions agitated to keep black people from working on the buses. In Coventry in 1955 the local transport union branch registered its opposition to the recruitment of black drivers and conductors. Despite persistent complaints from the Indian Workers' Association, the unions refused to budge. The TGWU branch responded sharply to the Asian workers' campaign. The branch chairman complained that the Indian Workers' Association was 'adopting a dictatorial attitude and eventually no doubt would like to rule the whole city' *(Coventry Evening Telegraph,* 3 November 1958).

Union officials tried to defuse the conflict by pretending that race was not the issue. They maintained that the union's bargaining position on wages and conditions was strengthened by running with a crew shortage. The TGWU's Midlands regional secretary Jack Jones (later to become the union's General Secretary) tried to reduce the dispute to a simple technical problem:

'The controversy is regretted...as I understand it the problem which arises relates only to the method of selection for employment.' *(Coventry Evening Telegraph,* 5 November 1958)

The reaction of the TGWU in Coventry was not an isolated one. In foundries, machine tool factories and in the car industry, shop steward committees demanded that black workers should be restricted to unskilled jobs. In 1961, for example, the shop steward committee at the Alfred Herbert machine tools factory in Coventry demanded restrictions on the promotion of black workers *(Coventry Evening Telegraph,* 21 October 1961). In the machine shop of an engineering firm in Keighley, 64 workers came out on strike when two Pakistanis were taken on as machine operators *(Telegraph and Argus,* 27 July 1961). A recent study of the post-war history of the textile industry in Bradford shows the extensive racial division of labour that was established with the complicity of the unions (see Ralph Fevre, *Cheap labour and racial discrimination).*

The unions cooperated in the enforcement of an informal colour bar in the labour market. In certain sectors — the docks, council manual departments, the print shops — vestiges of these colour bars still survive. In general, however, old patterns of fixed discrimination have given way to more subtle methods. The system of colour bars did not merely prevent the employment or promotion of black workers into skilled employment, it also ghettoised them into certain employment areas. It led, for example, to the widespread phenomenon of the 'all-black' night shift. The consequences of the persistence of these diverse forms of discrimination became clearer in the sixties and seventies as racist hostility grew in intensity.

White against black

The oppressive conditions faced by black workers and the indifference of union leaders to their plight inevitably provoked resistance. One of the first instances of the revolt of black workers took place at Red Scar Mills, part of the Courtauld textile and chemicals empire at Preston, Lancashire, in 1965. The dispute began over a new productivity deal negotiated between the Courtauld management and the transport workers' union which represented most of the production workers at the Preston plant. The deal meant that black workers in the spinning department had to work 50 per cent harder for a token extra hourly payment. The black workers, who were not even consulted about the deal, were already working under worse conditions than the rest of the workforce. After staging a sit down protest, 350 Indian and Pakistani workers came out on unofficial strike. Management was outraged — but so was the TGWU.

The union refused to support the strike and approved the use of scabs who worked overtime to keep the spinning department working at 85 per cent capacity. As far as the TGWU stewards were concerned this was not a 'normal' trade union dispute. 'The issues involved in the Courtauld's strike appear to be entirely racial', one steward told the local press *(Lancashire Evening Post,* 25 May 1965).

Vice-chairman of the factory-wide shop stewards' organisation, Richard Roberts, was a founding member of the Preston Commonwealth Unity Association and reputed to be on the far left of the Labour Party. Yet he took a racist stand against the strikers. He told one interviewer that the feeling of the union branch was that members were 'beginning to feel that

Room at the bottom: dead-end jobs and low pay for black workers

Not part of the union: black workers have fought their battles alone

we have done too much for immigrants'. He insisted that 'the strike had to be broken' and that 'they have got to learn the consequences of unofficial action; they have got to come back individually' (cited in John Torode, 'Race moves in on the unions', *New Society,* 17 June 1965).

The strike — the first in the history of Red Scar Mills — was over in three weeks, defeated by hostility from fellow workers and sabotaged by the union. After the strikers returned to work the tensions continued. At a mass meeting white workers demanded that management victimise 'black trouble-makers'. Workers in one department came out on a short strike to force management to pursue this policy.

Over the next decade more than 100 strikes like the one at Red Scar Mills took place. In almost every case the unions put the workers' demands down to language and communications problems. It became common currency in the trade union world to depict black strikers as workers suffering from an inability to adapt to the customs of British industrial relations. This was another way of saying that union officials saw black-led strikes as a threat to their white members. A few months after the Red Scar strike, black workers were told that they would have to be educated in the ways of British trade unionism. All the blame for racial tensions was put on the backs of the victims of racism. In fact, as one delegate told the 1965 TUC conference, black workers had a lot to be thankful for — not least the tolerance of their white brothers in the unions:

> **'Most of all, I want to congratulate the British working man on his tolerance and good humour and willingness to work alongside the coloured workers.' *(TUC Report,* 1965)**

With attitudes like this on display at the conferences of the labour movement, racist prejudices were allowed to flourish all the way down to workplace level. Another notorious strike took place at Imperial Typewriters in Leicester in 1974.

Once again the TGWU was the main union involved, but this time there was the added ingredient of National Front involvement 'from the boardroom downwards', according to local organiser Anthony Reed Herbert. The Asian workers — 1100 out of a total workforce of 1650 — came out on strike when they found that management had been cheating on their bonus payments. They were also demanding the right to elect their own shop stewards, which was not allowed under the union's bureaucratic procedures.

The National Front organised violent strike-breaking activities, and generally whipped the white workers into a racist frenzy. Alarmed at this state of affairs, senior TGWU officials intervened to try to cool things down. The strike was crushed and the factory shut down altogether shortly afterwards. Although they deplored the intervention of the National Front, the union officials constantly played into their hands. Local TGWU full-time official George Bromley spoke about the Asian strikers in terms difficult to distinguish from the fascists:

'They've got to learn to fit in with our ways, you know. We haven't got to fit in with theirs...in a civilised society, the majority view will prevail. Some people must learn how things are done.'(Interview with Radio Leicester, *Race Today,* October 1974)

According to Bromley it was a language problem; 'they can't understand very well or express themselves very well'. Leicester TGWU vice-chair Bill Batstone was even blunter:

'Sooner or later somebody had to stand up and be counted. The Asians cannot come here and make their own rules.' (Quoted in *Race Today,* September 1974).

The barely disguised racism of the unions contributed to the racial tensions on the factory floor and added to the isolation of the strikers that made their defeat inevitable.

The Imperial Typewriters' experience was repeated in less dramatic ways in hundreds of workplaces around the country. Black workers let down by their unions were left to face racial hostility alone. The trade union leadership is now eager to forget what happened at Mansfield Hosiery, Standard Telephone and Cable, Birmid Qualcast, Intex, Woolf's rubber factory, Perivale Gutterman, Harwood Cash Mill. In these and in countless other disputes black workers led the way — only to be left in the lurch by the official labour movement.

The TUC's conversion

In the early seventies, the labour bureaucracy began to shift its policy towards black workers. The main impetus for change came from the National Front. In the 1974 General Election and in a series of local elections the fascists showed that, in areas with high immigrant populations, they could successfully exploit the race issue to take large numbers of traditional Labour votes. Other factors also played a part in the TUC's change of line. Strikes like those at Red Scar Mill and Imperial Typewriters showed the disruptive effects of racism on industrial relations. When racial tensions exploded into open conflict, the stability and coherence of the unions was imperilled.

There was the additional danger that TUC indifference to or complicity in racism could alienate black workers from the unions. The spate of militant strikes led by black workers alerted the TUC to the need for rapid action. To show that it meant business, the TUC established its Equal Rights Committee in 1975 and later published its own guidelines — *Black workers: a charter for equality of opportunity.*

The TUC's anti-racist conversion was only skin deep. This was only to be expected given the bureaucracy's continuing attachment to the British state. As committed British nationalists, the TUC leaders never questioned the need for immigration controls and continued to look upon black workers as a potential source of instability. This outlook inevitably restricted the scope of the TUC's anti-racism. The TUC was quite prepared to concede that racism was a problem in society — so long as it did not have to admit that it was a problem inside the trade union movement. The bureaucrats' anti-racism meant objecting to National Front propaganda or blatant forms of discrimination by employers. It did not require them to tackle discrimination in workplace practices and inside the unions.

The trade union movement's anti-racist programme included three elements. First, the TUC called for a ban on National Front marches and meetings. Trade union officials continually emphasised this demand. However, the bureaucrats' preoccupation with the fascists arose more out of their concern to curb potential right-wing trouble-makers inside the unions than from any commitment to fighting racism. The TUC's Equal Rights Committee chair Tom Jackson freely admitted that the TUC was more worried by the National Front than by the problems of racism:

> **'It is unfortunate that the National Front had to stimulate the action because we could have dealt with it more rationally and could perhaps have prevented the rise of the National Front.'**

The second aspect of the TUC's programme was to make frequent exhortations about multi-racial harmony. This was less a solution than wishful thinking — a pious expression of the desire that the problems of racism would go away. Its third solution — the most hypocritical of all — was to appeal to black workers to join unions. The percentage of black workers organised in trade unions has always been higher than that of white workers. The TUC's appeal absolved the union leaders of their responsibility for workplace racism and by implication shifted the blame on to non-unionised black workers. Yet campaigns to recruit blacks to the unions remained a central feature of the TUC's anti-racist rhetoric throughout the seventies.

In 1978, after the series of violent racist attacks in East London, TUC General Secretary Len Murray went down to Brick Lane to tell local Bangladeshis to join the unions:

'The trade union movement in the East End has a distinguished record of working for equal opportunity for all workers of whatever religions or ethnic background. We hope that they in turn will, by joining and working in their trade unions, help us to help them combat the evil they are facing.' (TUC statement, *Race relations in East London,* 1978)

It was far from clear what Murray proposed to do to counter racist violence. He warned against taking 'violent action', reminding the victims of racist terror that 'the police have a difficult job'. More than a year later the South East Region of the TUC got around to launching a 'major campaign against racism'. This turned out to be a recruitment campaign aimed primarily at black workers.

Over the past five years the TUC has built up its anti-racist profile. It has produced numerous leaflets and pamphlets promoting the desirability of a multi-racial society. After the 1981 riots, the TUC rushed out a document, entitled *Regenerating our inner cities,* to demonstrate its concern over the plight of black youth. The TUC now talks of the need for 'positive discrimination' and arranges language classes. Every trade union conference now resounds with obligatory declarations about the evils of racism. Yet the TUC still has nothing to say about the main sphere of racial discrimination where trade union action could be effective — the workplace.

As far as the TUC is concerned racism within its own ranks is not a problem. Whenever racial incidents in the workplace are brought to public attention, union leaders pretend that race is not the issue. For example, at Ford's Dagenham plant, where there have been numerous arguments and fights between white supervisors and black production workers, shop stewards and trade union officials go to great lengths to deny any racial aspect to the conflicts (See *Daily Mail,* 7 June 1978 and *The Observer,* 23 July 1978). Union officials make similar protestations today when it is suggested that the exclusion of blacks from council manual departments did not come about spontaneously but as a result of trade union complicity.

A divided class

The TUC would prefer to ignore the recent introduction of race checks into the public services. Yet the implementation of race checks in hospitals and dole offices requires the active cooperation of public service trade unionists. Here is a blatant form of racial discrimination which the unions could easily render inoperable. For the TUC this is all the more reason to duck the whole issue and stick to sermonising about multi-racial harmony.

The trade unions are prepared to organise black workers and to collect their union dues. In return the TUC sings the praises of a multi-racial Britain and passes resolutions expressing its fervent belief in racial equality. In practice black workers receive nothing useful from their unions. They are union members but they are not considered part of the British labour movement. At root this is because of the ideological bond between the trade unions and the British state. Together with the employers, the trade union leaders argue that British industry must come first and that the national interest must be defended. This nationalist prejudice assists the bosses but divides the labour movement. Workers see themselves as British first and workers second. That is why chauvinist attacks on foreigners — including foreign workers — are accepted in the labour movement.

The informal colour bar perpetuated through the unions divides the working class. It leads to the isolation of black workers and to the erosion of the basic principles of class unity. It also means that the working class, the one social force that has a direct interest in fighting racism, itself becomes infected by it. The main beneficiaries of racial divisions are the employers. It is not merely a question of divide and rule. The capitalist class knows that in racism it has a powerful instrument that cuts across all classes and helps consolidate social support for its policies.

7. The great evasion

Like the TUC, the British anti-racist movement has always been highly selective in its anti-racism. The left has conducted many anti-racist campaigns, but — with the exception of Workers Against Racism — it has studiously ignored three crucial issues. First, the left has done virtually no campaigning against immigration controls. Even the few half-hearted protests it has launched on this question have not been directed at immigration controls as such, but against particular pieces of legislation, such as the 1971 Immigration Act or the recent Nationality Act. Second, the left has neglected the problem of racist violence. Third, the issue of racism in the workplace has become a taboo subject. A reluctance to embarrass trade union leaders and a general inability to challenge everyday racism have rendered the left incapable of taking up problems of discrimination and prejudice in employment and working practices. The selective approach of left-wing anti-racism has narrowed the scope of the anti-racist movement and prevented an effective fight against racism in the working class. To appreciate how the British anti-racist movement came to adopt such a restrictive approach it is useful to examine the assumptions that underlie its campaigns.

Anti-racism and the state

In chapter 6 we showed how the close links between the labour bureaucracy and the British state shaped the trade unions' attitude towards immigrant workers. The official labour movement's strong attachment to the capitalist state has also influenced the views of the British left. The left's loyalty to the state lies at the root of its inability to conduct a systematic fight against racism.

Significant sections of the left look upon state institutions as potential instruments for fighting racism. Of course, it is widely recognised that the police, the courts, the Home Office and many other state agencies enforce or actively promote racism. But the conduct of these agencies can easily be explained as the result of the activities of individual racist officers or officials, or as the consequence of Tory laws which can be thrown out as soon as there is an anti-racist majority in Parliament. The left has singled out as racist certain forms of state activity (Special Patrol Group raids, particular deportations) and certain laws (the 'sus' laws, the 1971 Immigration Act, the 1981 Nationality Act). Other aspects of state activity are either ıgnored (immigration raids, special detention centres, criminalisation of black youth) or portrayed in a neutral or even positive light (community policing, police committees, the incorporation of anti-racist campaigns on to the state payroll).

The left divides up the state machinery into its supposedly 'racist' and 'non-racist' and even 'anti-racist' components. The SPG is racist, community policing is OK. Tory immigration laws are discriminatory, but Labour immigration laws could be colour blind. Faith in the state is so strong that anti-racists have no inhibitions about asking the state to fight racism. Anti-racists can even be heard demanding that the police set an example by rooting out racists from their own ranks. It is not uncommon for far left groups to invite or approve state bans on demonstrations by racists and fascists. Left wingers at the North London Polytechnic ran a campaign throughout 1983 and 1984 to get the authorities to ban a National Front student from attending lectures at the college. The left is so blinded by its illusions in the state that it is happy to hand over the job of fighting racism to the British establishment.

From a working class point of view, the state cannot be divided into its nasty and pleasant sides. For Marxists the state is an instrument of class domination, whether this is exercised through the iron fist of the Metropolitan Police's Instant Response Units or through the smooth talkers of the race relations industry. No state institution can fight racism for the simple reason that it is through the state that racial oppression is enforced.

Immigration control

Immigration controls make racism respectable. They provide the legal framework for racial oppression. Immigration controls are divisive and discriminatory by their very nature. They divide the working class into first class and second class citizens. Further, they are measures introduced by the state to control the movement of the working class. The consequences of immigration controls go far beyond the mere regulation of movement in and out of the country. Immigration laws emphasise workers' nationality and help to foster a climate in which patriotic and chauvinist values can flourish.

Marxists have long recognised the reactionary character of immigration controls. At the 1907 International Socialist Congress in Stuttgart, left wingers opposed right-wing attempts to justify immigration regulations. Lenin, who led the opposition on behalf of the Russian Bolshevik Party, later summed up the debate:

'On the question of emigration and immigration, a clear difference of opinion arose between the opportunists and the revolutionaries in the Commission of the Stuttgart Congress. The opportunists cherished the idea of limiting the right of migration of backward, undeveloped workers — especially the Japanese and the Chinese. In the minds of these opportunists the spirit of narrow craft isolation, of trade union exclusiveness, outweighed the consciousness of socialist tasks: work of educating and organising those strata of the proletariat which have not yet been drawn into the labour movement.' (VI Lenin, 'International Socialist Congress in Stuttgart', *Collected Works,* volume 13)

During his exile in Switzerland, Lenin observed how the capitalist class there relied on hostility against foreign workers to maintain its domination over the entire working class. Lenin renewed his opposition to immigration regulations and called upon the labour movement to make solidarity with immigrant workers its top priority:

'It is necessary, first, constantly and unswervingly to fight for organisational rapprochement between foreign and Swiss workers bringing them together in the same unions, and for their complete equality (civic and political). The specific feature of imperialism in Switzerland is precisely the increasing exploitation of disenfranchised foreign workers by the Swiss bourgeoisie, which bases its hopes on estrangement between these two categories of workers.' (VI Lenin, 'Tasks of left Zimmerwaldists', *Collected Works,* volume 23)

In its early days the British anti-racist movement was hostile to immigration controls. In September 1961 the Coordinating Committee Against Racial Discrimination organised a demonstration in Birmingham against the government's new Immigration Bill. Apart from a demonstration in London in 1969, the Birmingham protest was more or less the first and last attempt to fight against all forms of immigration controls. After the enactment of the 1961 Immigration Bill, the British left made its peace with immigration controls. This change of line was particularly striking in the case of the Labour Party. In the early sixties the party had roundly condemned the Tories' legislation as racist and upheld an 'open door' policy. Yet by 1964 Roy Hattersley had reversed his position. He was now of the opinion that 'unrestricted immigration can only produce additional problems'. The rest of the Parliamentary Labour Party more or less agreed.

Most anti-racists did not go as far as Hattersley. Instead they launched a quest for the illusory goal of a 'non-racist' immigration policy. The Communist Party devoted much energy to this futile endeavour. In 1978, for example, the *Morning Star* agreed that the state had 'the right to regulate immigration and emigration', but 'not by racist criteria' (20 June). Other left wingers invented all sorts of justifications for the right of the capitalist state to divide the working class. For the Labour left paper *Tribune,* immigration control was desirable because it was a form of planning:

'Socialists who see the need for economic and social planning cannot be expected to argue for free movement of labour in a capitalist international economy, and be condemned as racist if they refuse to do so.' (26 May 1978)

The Labour Party's 1982 programme was more straightforward — it justified controls by the requirements of the capitalist economy.

Alex Lyon, the Labour left's spokesman on race in the late seventies, became a fervent champion of non-racist immigration controls. The rest of the left was not far behind and the fictitious distinction between racist and non-racist immigration controls was generally accepted. The 1971 Immigration Act was singled out for special attention while the legitimacy of the principle of immigration controls was put beyond question. Attempts to fight all immigration controls were condemned as either hopelessly unrealistic or insensitive to nationalist sensibilities. Communist Party national organiser Dave Cook expressed the prevailing wisdom of the left in the late seventies:

'All of us on the left understand that unemployment and worsening social services result from the economic crisis of British capitalism. However the "no immigration controls" position puts forward a demand which can easily create the impression that the left are oblivious to these problems.' *(Morning Star,* 20 June 1978)

Cook's capitulation to the pressures of British chauvinism typified the left's approach to the immigration issue. Even the more radical left-wing organisations — the Socialist Workers' Party and other factions — chose to take the pragmatic road. They either ignored the issue of immigration controls or affiliated to the Campaign Against Racist Laws. The function of this campaign was to provide its affiliates with anti-racist credentials. It was a consummate practitioner of the racist/non-racist immigration laws double standard. It denounced the Tory Nationality Act and maintained a diplomatic silence on the fact that the Act had been drawn up largely by the preceding Labour government. The campaign's most dramatic gesture was to organise a demonstration against the Nationality Act—two months after it had come into operation.

Evasion of the issue of immigration controls represents a concession to racism. Those who fail to question the principle of immigration control are in no position to fight other forms of discrimination. Acquiescing to immigration controls means playing by the rules drawn up by the state. A recent academic survey praises the Joint Council for the Welfare of Immigrants because its 'leadership have assiduously tried to steer the organisation away from taking a position on political issues (such as the principle of immigration control) which might seriously have divided it' (M Fitzgerald, *Political parties and black people).* The problem is that it is impossible to fight racism without taking a political position in opposition to immigration controls. 'Non-political' opponents of deportations are reduced to making humanitarian pleas or trying to score fine legal points. While sensible and realistic anti-racists plead for special exemptions, the racist politics behind immigration controls are allowed unchallenged sway over British society.

At peace with the police

The attachment to the state that leads the left to accept immigration controls also leads it to equivocate on the issue of policing. Everybody knows that the British police are racist. Even establishment bodies like the Policy Studies Institute have commented on the prevalence of racist prejudice inside the police force. Black people know from first-hand experience that racist policing is not an occasional abuse but an everyday feature of law and order in British society.

The left, however, takes a more equivocal line on the police. The dominant perspective among radical anti-racists is not to condemn and expose the police force but to try to reform it. The left recognises the legitimacy of police repression but wants it to be exercised in a non-racist way. To realise this objective the left proposes that policing becomes more community oriented and more accountable. A recent GLC booklet sums up the left's commitment to building up public trust in the police:

'Effective policing depends on there being a basic level of trust beween the community and the police. Unfortunately this does not always exist with

regard to some of London's black and other ethnic minorities.'(GLC, *London against racism)*

The best that can be said of the desire to establish trust between the police and the black community is that it is naive. The worst is that this approach sustains the illusion that the enforcers of racial oppression can be made accountable to those whom they oppress. In reality, the police are accountable to only one section of society — their paymasters in the capitalist state. Community policing can never be more than a sham to soften up the victims of state repression. Community policemen have demonstrated their usefulness in inner-city ghettos and in pit villages during the 1984 miners' strike. They can finger local activists to be picked up by the heavy squads. Both the establishment and the left want 'effective policing' — on this point there is no controversy. What the left wants is a reformed non-racist police force on which it could rely to fight racism.

The left's attitude towards the police may seem bizarre. It is obvious to anybody that the police are thoroughly racist. So why bother trying to reform an inherently irreformable institution? The answer is that, despite all their criticisms of police conduct, anti-racists look upon the police as potential allies. Just as the left asks the state to ban fascists, so it implores the police to fight racism.

Racist violence

The left has consistently condemned racist violence. Yet it has equally consistently and with equal vehemence denounced those who organise physical resistance to racist attacks. The left has used different arguments to justify its passivity towards racist violence. In February 1981 Peter Hain, then the press officer for the Anti-Nazi League, argued that the aim of the League ought to be to 'broaden the basis' of its support and that the issue of community self-defence is one which would undoubtedly injure the breadth of support' *(Searchlight,* February 1981). A month later Hain went a step further — it was no longer merely inopportune to fight racist thugs, it was now declared wrong in principle:

'The one thing we're not getting into is a counter-terrorist operation. I think that would be politically wrong, morally unacceptable. I think it would be totally counter-productive.' *(New Musical Express,* 7 March 1981)

The left's condemnation of resistance against racist violence stems from the liberal politics of British anti-racism. In effect, the field of battle is abandoned to the racist thugs. When British anti-racists are not evading the issue of racist violence they assign responsibility for fighting it to the police. Thus racist attacks are followed by a chorus of pleas for police action. Imploring the racist police to do something about racist violence is one of the most grotesque features of the anti-racist movement.

The dead end of British anti-racism was strikingly revealed in London in 1984. While the GLC spent millions on its 'anti-racist year', violent attacks on black people, particularly in East London, carried on as usual. The Labour left seemed to find it easier to fight racism in the council chamber and on the advertising billboards than on the streets of the capital. While the left celebrated 'anti-racist year' at County Hall, Asian families lived in a state of siege on GLC housing estates in East London. Behind the scenes, GLC-funded anti-racist groups attempted to defuse the situation by transferring Asian families from the troubled housing estates back to the ghettos.

The only attempt to fight back against the wave of racist terror was organised by East London Workers Against Racism. This initiative was immediately denounced by the state-funded anti-racist groups. In a joint letter they evaded responsibility for fighting racist terror by arguing that the right of individual families to move should be respected:

'If the family wants to move, this should be respected — it may be a victory for the racists if they are transferred but it is also a victory for the racists when someone gets beaten up.' *(London Housing,* November 1984)

By putting the onus on the victims of racist attacks the quango anti-racists ignored the basic problem that as long as racist violence remains unchallenged families will understandably want to move. When nothing is done to resist racist thugs, violence becomes a problem that each family in isolation has to come to terms with and transfer indeed becomes the only solution.

The left's defeatist response to racist violence is the most striking consequence of its subservience to the state. It is not surprising that racist violence has become an embarrassing subject for a movement that resigns itself to asking the police to fight back on its behalf.

Pious platitudes

Anti-racism has become a movement of moralism and platitudes, appealing to the British tradition of 'fair play' and liberalism. In the tradition of nineteenth century liberalism, the left hopes that through education and example racist ideas can be neutralised. From the Anti-Nazi League to the GLC-inspired campaigns against racist advertising, the problem is treated in the patronising style of the liberal do-gooder. The GLC's posters warn that racism is not good for you and council officials

GLC

Greater London Council
Housing Department

Director of Housing
L Bennett OBE FRICS FIH
District Housing Manager P.F.J.RYRIE., MIH
Eastern District Office
723 Commercial Road London E14 7LD

Telephone 01-987 5060
Please reply to the District Housing Manager
My reference HG/D32/DDHM/LWH
Your reference
Date 4 June 1984

Mr. Tahid,

London, E.3.

Dear Mr. Tahid,

I understand that when you called at this office on 1 June to enquire about your transfer prospects, you adopted a very offensive and threatening attitude towards our Housing Welfare Officer, Mr. Rahman, who has in fact been doing his best to help you and has made a very substantial and useful report on your case. I want to make it clear that behaviour of this kind is not acceptable in this District – or, indeed, in England generally. I am giving you the opportunity to apologise for your conduct and to undertake not to repeat it; I hope you will take that opportunity in replying to this letter.

Yours sincerely,

GLC

Greater London Council
Housing Department

Head of Housing Services
B R Steele MA PhD
District Housing Manager
P F J Ryrie MIH

Eastern District Office
723 Commercial Road London E14 7LD

Telephone 01-987 5060
Please reply to the District Housing Manager
My reference HG/D32/DDHM/LWH
Your reference
Date 18 September 1984

Mr. A. Tahid.

Bow,
London, E.3.

Dear Mr. Tahid,

Your complaint of racial harassment has been very carefully investigated by the Council's officers and there seems no doubt that you have suffered such harassment at various times. However, the trouble now appears to have ceased and it is to be hoped that you will now be able to live reasonably peacably and securely. In the circumstances the awarding of extra priority for a transfer cannot be justified but your transfer application remains on record and your case will be reviewed three months from now.

In the meantime, our estate officer will watch the situation most carefully; if you have any further trouble, please do not hesitate to let him know.

Yours sincerely,

L. W. HUDSON
Deputy District Housing Manager

GLC
Working for housing in London

Sermons: the GLC's commitment to fighting racism is empty rhetoric are advised to take up courses on 'racial awareness'.

The left entirely ignores the roots of racism in capitalist society. Indeed, it believes that the state which enforces capitalist social relations can be used to fight racism. The left's deference to the state is the fatal flaw in its desire to combat racism. Unless the struggle against racism is fought from an anti-capitalist point of view it becomes ineffective and divisive. That is why the struggle must be based on the working class, the main social force with a vital interest in fighting the system.

Instead of trying to build a movement inside the working class, left-wing anti-racists have ignored the working class altogether. The left has done nothing to challenge racism on the factory floor. Most anti-racists are reluctant to stir things in the unions and thus embarrass the labour bureaucrats. In return for this understanding approach the union leaders have been happy to issue resolutions and reports condemning racism and supporting anti-racist initiatives, so long as they steer clear of the labour movement. State-funded anti-racist campaigners would rather deal with union bureaucrats than with working class people. They both speak the same language and share a common psychology and outlook. Both are convinced that their dedicated campaign for racial justice is being thwarted by selfish and prejudiced trade union members. In private they also shake their heads wearily over the activities of some black people whose anger and impatience sometimes upsets the officials' carefully devised schemes.

The anti-racist movement's indifference to the working class leads it to formulate a set of policies which are designed to stir the liberal conscience. That is why they are so ineffective. On important political issues people are moved by class interests, not by appeals for fair play. Liberal anti-racism is made up of platitudes that nobody can disagree with, but which nobody will act upon. The anti-racist movement thrives on sermons about racial harmony and equality, but turns a blind eye to racial violence and the degradation of immigration controls. The classless approach of the radical anti-racist movement has failed to confront the divisions between black and white workers in Britain. It has done nothing to help overcome the isolation of black people. After more than 10 years of left-wing anti-racist campaigning, black people are still largely forced to fight alone.

8. The way ahead

Racism is more influential in British society than ever before. Yet the anti-racist movement has become neutralised through its involvement with state-funded agencies. Black people can expect little from the organised labour movement and are forced to fight back on their own. The recession has contributed to the build-up of racial oppression and the position of black people in society continues to deteriorate.

Although black people bear the brunt of oppression, racism also has a damaging impact on other workers. Racism is not only divisive — it also helps to demoralise the working class. The chauvinist prejudices that permeate the British labour movement are a formidable barrier to its emancipation. Racist propaganda turns worker against worker and rallies large numbers of workers behind the banner of reaction. The British establishment relies on nationalist prejudices to divide and disorient the labour movement. Up to now it has played the racist card with remarkable success.

The establishment responds to every expression of working class vitality with a barrage of chauvinist propaganda. Politicians and employers appeal to trade unionists to moderate their demands 'in the national interest'. When strikes break out the bosses invoke the threat of foreign competition. The 'Falklands Factor', which united all true Britons in a wave of jingo fever against 'the Argies' in 1982, provided the establishment with its model campaign for the eighties. It was used systematically against the miners during the 1984 strike. For Thatcher and the media, the miners became 'the enemy within' who threatened the national interest through their violent picketing and their defiance of the courts. Gutter press journalists filled out parallels between the miners' leader Arthur Scargill and former Argentinian leader Galtieri with allegations about links between the miners and the IRA, Libya's Colonel Gadaffi and Moscow gold.

The British establishment can get away with playing the racist card because it knows that many influential figures in the labour movement share its chauvinist prejudices. Too often trade union activists and Labour left politicians put forward a radical nationalist perspective as a way of fighting for workers' interests. Instead of rejecting patriotism as the ideology of the bosses, labour leaders try to appropriate it for their own ends. When the Tory government removed trade union rights from workers employed at its GCHQ spy centre at Cheltenham, union leaders protested that this was an insult to the patriotism of their members. Trade unionists went on protest marches wearing their war medals to show that their devotion to the nation was second to none. Union leaders were even prepared to give an undertaking not to go on strike in the interests of upholding national security at GCHQ. The government simply laughed and demanded that workers give up their unions altogether in the cause of national security. Trade unionism at GCHQ was smashed.

The labour movement's approach to the GCHQ issue was consistent with its wider outlook. Even left-wing Labour politicians are imbued with a radical patriotic outlook that is often hostile to everything foreign. Instead of concentrating its fire on the home grown British ruling class, the left prefers to denounce the evils of foreign multinationals or the EEC. Trade union militants often go along with their bosses' preoccupations with foreign competitors and demand import controls on goods produced abroad. During the miners' strike many union militants tried to make an issue of the American origins of the chairman of the National Coal Board. The British bosses on the board were compared favourably to Ian MacGregor, the 'American import'. As long as this sort of nationalist prejudice is so influential on the left wing of the labour movement, the bosses will be confident that they can play the racist card with impunity.

Workers will not be able to act as an independent force until they shake off the chauvinist outlook they have taken over from the bosses. Because racism unites workers with their bosses it leads to the paralysis of independent action. Employers could never convince workers that their interests are the same in matters of wages and working conditions. Every trade unionist recognises the boss as an opponent across the negotiating table or factory or office floor. But when it comes to wider questions of foreign competition or foreign immigrants, the employers know that they can rely on their workers' support. The employers feel secure in the knowledge that on these key issues they can win the loyalty of those whom they confront in wage bargaining. Thus, racism goes much further than its effect on the relations between black and white people. It also leads the labour movement to accept national rather than class solutions to political problems.

It is impossible to fight the Tories — or any section of the British establishment — unless reactionary sentiments are curbed within the labour movement. It is easy enough to dismiss the racist Tory backwoodsmen. But it is much more difficult to isolate the nationalist rhetoric of left-wing labour bureaucrats. Yet unless this is done, the hold of the ruling class over those it exploits will remain as strong as ever. Fighting racism is not something to be left for some future date but a precondition for taking the first step forward as an independent class. When the working class takes the side of the oppressed this will be a sign that a new independent working class movement is in the making.

The fight against racism cannot be restricted to a campaign against racist ideas. It has to be directed against the practical manifestations of the problem. Because racial oppression is enforced and legitimised through the capitalist state, the perspective the working class adopts towards the state determines the effectiveness of its anti-racist campaigning. Once it is accepted that the state has the right to impose immigration controls, then discrimination can become the norm in every sphere of life. Oppressive laws require practical implementation. Police attacks on black people are not incidental, they are an essential feature of law enforcement. State racism underpins chauvinist ideology and provides a framework for everyday racism. Every racist thug on the street carries the state's official seal of approval.

The diverse manifestations of racism cannot be fought in isolation because behind the racist thug, the racist policeman, the racist Home Office or the racist housing department official stand the institutions of the racist state. These institutions sustain the racist consensus that pervades British society. As long as these institutions retain their legitimacy, racist views will continue to prevail throughout society. Challenging racist sentiments without taking on the state means treating the symptoms but ignoring the cause. This has been the central weakness of British anti-racism. Everyday discrimination cannot be fought without tackling its institutional foundations. The working class cannot root out racism unless it opposes all immigration controls.

The British establishment understands the key role of immigration laws and attaches considerable importance to them. Even today, when primary immigration has virtually ceased, the establishment still makes a great fuss about a few immigrants who want to join their relatives in Britain. This shows that this legislation is not merely concerned about the numbers of potential immigrants. Its central significance is to serve as a symbol of British nationhood — as a reminder of the privilege of being British and an implicit invitation to defend these privileges. The break-up of thousands of Asian families is a small price to pay for consolidating the patriotic consensus. Racism cannot be fought without challenging this consensus. Individual patriots may be well meaning, polite and inoffensive to black people. But British patriotism means loyalty to a ruthless and oppressive imperialist power. British nationalism is racist to the core — and this is not just because of Britain's imperialist past, but because of its imperialist present. That's why opposition to immigration controls is a precondition for effective anti-racist action.

State discrimination must be fought at every level. Passport checks and raids should be resisted on the grounds that the state has no right to interfere in the life of the working class. Deportations must be actively opposed, not through pleading and petitioning, but through challenging the right of the state to tell workers where they can stay, when and for how long. Deportation laws cannot be used for anti-racist ends, they must be made inoperable by mass resistance.

Far from relying on state agencies, an effective anti-racist movement must vigorously oppose the activities of all state institutions from the Metropolitan Police to the Commission for Racial Equality. The most effective response to racism is the formation of workers' defence groups. Only organised workers have the power to run racist thugs off the streets and every worker has a duty to defend the working class against racists.

Today most anti-racists see the police as a practical alternative to workers' defence groups. This is a dangerous delusion. From time to time the police may react against the more extreme manifestations of racist terror. But the police enforce the racist laws of the British state as part of their daily routine. Their incapacity to fight racism is confirmed by the experience of thousands of black people who have appealed to them for help only to be harassed and asked to produce their passports. Rather than being part of the solution, the police are very much part of the problem. But are workers' defence groups a realistic alternative?

Every blow struck against oppression or exploitation meets with the organised violence of the ruling class. Most of the time working class people are not prepared for this show of force and suffer the consequences. Sooner or later the alternative becomes either to abandon the struggle or to organise against the violence of the state. If the miners had not taken elementary steps to defend themselves against police violence during the early months of 1984, their strike would have been smashed at an early stage. Measures which were regarded as irrelevant at the beginning of the strike became a practical necessity after a few months. The same principle applies to the struggle against racism.

It is not a question of whether anti-racist defence groups are realistic or

We want action! Workers Against Racism demonstration outside the 1982 TUC

not. The point is that racism cannot be fought effectively without the independent organisation of the working class. Racial oppression leads to racial violence, whether it is conducted by the state or by individual racists. To ignore this violence is to renounce the struggle against racism altogether. For too long anti-racists have lived on a staple diet of petitions, lobbies and paper campaigns. In the meantime little effective action has been taken to assist and defend black people from racist violence. The time has come to cut out the rhetoric and begin to organise workers' defence groups. A prerequisite for realising this objective is the organisation of anti-racist work inside the labour movement.

Anti-racist action must begin by forcing the issue inside the labour movement. Active trade unionists must set an example by crushing racism inside the unions. We cannot fight racism effectively unless we cleanse our own ranks first. To denounce Tory racism while ignoring racism inside the labour movement is an act of hypocrisy which does a disservice to the anti-racist cause. It is also short-sighted because unless working class people are mobilised against racism not much can be achieved.

There is no point in just talking about unity between black and white workers. Unity cannot be declared — it has to be fought for. The onus rests upon white workers to set an example through fighting oppression. This must be done, not as a favour to black people, but as a matter of necessity for the survival of the entire working class. Through the experience of fighting against the state, workers will learn how to fight as an independent class.